Embrace

Stories of humour, humanness, and hope

Inspired and illustrated by Madeline Kean

Written by

LISA WALLACE

Tellwell Talent
www.tellwell.ca

ISBN
978-0-2288-1459-7 (Hardcover)
978-0-2288-1458-0 (Paperback)
978-0-2288-1460-3 (eBook)

Gratitudes

Maddy – Without you, there would be no book. Without you, I wouldn't be half the parent that I am. I learn from you not only daily but sometimes hourly. You embrace bravery at every turn. Thank you for the courage to share these stories and for your works of art for the cover and throughout this book.

Lauren – I am grateful to have a child who understands my imperfections as a parent and has learned to embrace the gifts of her sister. Thank you for the belly laughs as we reminisced and wrote this book.

Kieran – I couldn't have asked for a better bonus son. Thank you for embracing me as your bonus mom. Thank you for your creativity with the cover design of this book.

Scott – Thank you for embracing the daily learning with me and for always being supportive of what I want to try. Love you.

Mom – Thank you for being the consistent, caring adult in my childhood who led me through some of my most challenging times. You continue to be my cheerleader, shoulder and sounding board.

Brenda – Thank you for organizing girls' weekends and getaways to help keep me grounded and remind me of my role as sister! You are not only my sister, you are my friend.

Leslee – More than cousins, we are friends. Thank you for sharing your expertise and for the many conversations about the world of people with diverse abilities and for being there when I needed to bounce ideas off you.

Susan – You are my best friend and you embraced the role of 'auntie' for my girls from the day they were born and for that I am eternally grateful.

Mark and Tania – Thank you for being great co-parents with Scott and me. Maddy would not have had the rich experiences in her life without the four of us embracing the journey together.

Suzanne – You always embrace the time you spend with Maddy learning about the social world, with compassion and humour. For that we are grateful.

Dr. Lippa - Thank you for always making the time to guide us through the medical world, and for embracing our questions with patience and honesty. We appreciate you being on this journey with us.

Our medical community - We so appreciate the services we have received from the wide array of specialists within our region. We embrace each appointment as an opportunity to learn about the latest research, and that information helps guide us through our next decisions.

Our school community - Thank you for being "partners in learning" with our family. We are grateful to be able to embrace the learning as a team!

Embrace by Madeline Kean

E xpress yourself

M ake the most of each day – be grateful

B ravery builds confidence

R eslience is a choice

A lways believe in yourself

C ourage comes from within

E verybody deserves a joyful life

Although I had been note-taking and compiling this book for months, I came up with its title while I was at an orthotist appointment with my daughter, Maddy.

Maddy has been wearing orthotics in her shoes since she was five. For the past number of years, she has also been wearing soft ankle braces each day to keep her ankles stable and to help her walk with a more fluid gait. Throughout these same years, our orthopedic surgeon at British Columbia's Children's Hospital had recommended an ankle/foot orthotic (AFO). The AFO is a hard brace that runs from knee to ankle. It is hinged at the ankle then attaches to her foot (see her sketch of it on the back cover). It is cumbersome and obvious, but it was the next level of support to enable her to walk as easily as possible. I was hoping to put off the use of that brace for as long as possible, as I was worried about my daughter having yet one more thing to contend when it came to fitting in. Putting off the brace came from a well-intentioned place of protection but deep down, I knew better. Fitting in is about becoming what others want you to be – being accepted for being like everyone else rather than for being you. All along, however, Maddy strongly advocated for the AFO. She knew it would help her and didn't care if it was big and bulky or if she was going to fit in. She stood strong and said, "I need this brace. It is going to help me!" She was **embracing** her diverse abilities. In fact, when it came time to choose the colour for the plastic piece, she did not choose something muted that would blend in with her skin tone; she chose her favourite colour—purple—with her favourite pattern, horses! When the orthotist suggested that she could wear it under her pants or tights, Maddy bravely responded with, "Or I could wear it over top!"

Maddy has never been embarrassed about not being like everyone else. She has always accepted who she was even when others were not ready to. She has never put a limit on what she can do, and that has led us to learn from her in the most profound ways. It was on the day of the orthotist appointment that I started to connect with what author Brene Brown wrote about wholehearted living and how our life with Madeline has followed that path. Rather than focusing on fitting in with a group, we have tried to find communities of belonging for Maddy so that she could be accepted for her gifts rather than changing who she was because of them.

My name is Lisa Ball. It's also Lisa Kean. As well as Lisa Wallace.

I was born Lisa Ball in Chilliwack, BC. At the time, Chilliwack was an agricultural town. My parents owned a dairy equipment business, but I would not have called myself a farmer. I knew a lot about farming because of the way my dad spent time with me and my sister - taking us on service calls to local farms on Saturday mornings. I used to hang out in the milking parlours while my dad 'chewed the fat' with the farmers. Although I didn't love the manure smell of the parlour, I did get a view into what it was like to love your job. My dad was in his glory when he was problem-solving with the farmers and fixing their milking equipment. I learned perspective, patience and not to stand too close to the back end of a cow!

I went through school in Chilliwack and during those years, I moved two times. The first move was when my parents divorced in 1980. I was one of two students in my elementary school who had parents who were divorced. The divorce epidemic hadn't yet hit our small town and I really lost my sense of belonging at that time. My mom lost all of her 'couple friends' and became quite isolated. There was a noticeable shift in her social currency.

We went from being a family where we could afford most of the things we wanted, to a reduced income, single-parent family where my mom worked three jobs. We had to think about where our money was being spent. Times were lean for the remainder of my school years. I remember having to choose between spending money on a school field trip or ordering hot lunch – things that we would never have given a second thought to before the divorce.

Despite the struggles we had financially, my mom was my biggest champion. In the world of education, we say that every student needs to be connected to one caring adult who believes in them. My mom was that person. Because of her belief in me I always believed I could do anything I put my mind to. I knew I was not going to let myself be a product of my circumstances but rather a product of my possibilities. My will to be more than my circumstances has always guided me.

I graduated from high school in 1986 and had plans to attend the college in Chilliwack, but those plans changed when my mom got a job in Vancouver, about an hour and a half away. It would have been too taxing for her to spend three hours commuting round trip from Chilliwack to downtown Vancouver every day so we made the move to the city. I ended up going to a college in Vancouver and then transferred to the University of British Columbia (UBC) where I received my bachelor's degree in psychology and then my bachelor of education degree. I settled in nicely to Vancouver and had hoped to stay there to begin my career as a teacher, but the economy of the time had other plans for me. Getting a teaching contract in 1992 was an elusive thing. There was a hiring freeze in many school districts especially in those close to a metropolitan area like Vancouver. I started making my way east with my resume and in a twist of fate, I was hired by the Chilliwack school district! I am forever grateful for that hire as I have had numerous career opportunities within our district and have received tremendous support for our family.

Two months after I was hired by the Chilliwack school district to work as a TTOC (teacher teaching on call, also known as a substitute teacher), I was interviewed for a position teaching kindergarten. The vice-principal of the administration team that was interviewing me was Scott Wallace. The day after my hour-long interview, he called to offer me a halftime kindergarten teaching job. I was thrilled beyond belief to have my first contract! This meant financial stability for me as I was just starting out and wanted to plant my feet solidly on the ground. Scott and I only worked together for eight months but during that time we became great friends. He was a single dad with a son named Kieran and we spent a lot of time together hanging out with friends. We used to joke that we were the male and female version of the same person because we were so similar in our outlooks on life. We never dated each other, though. In fact, it was Scott who introduced me to Mark Kean. Scott was having a get-together one night and told me that I should come and meet his friend Mark because he thought we might hit it off together. All three of us were teachers at the time and so that was our common ground.

After chatting with Mark that evening at the party, I agreed to go climb one of our toughest mountains on the outskirts of Chilliwack the next day. Our relationship grew over the next year and a bit, and in 1996 I married Mark and became Lisa Kean. Mark was 10 years older than me so we wasted no time having children.

Lauren, who was born in 1997, 10 months after our wedding, is now 22 years old and has graduated from university. When she was born, Mark was over the moon. Lauren was challenging as a baby because she had colic and caused us many sleepless nights. Through her early toddler years, she was what we came to call 'spirited'. Parenting her required a lot of thinking so that she always felt like she had a choice in whatever it was we were asking of her. I just kept telling myself that although it took a lot of energy to parent a spirited child, it would benefit her when it came to those times in her life when she had to stand up for herself or to be a leader. We were right! Life settled down as she entered elementary school and she did not go through a rebellious stage as a teenager. I always saw us as having two children but when Lauren was exhibiting her 'spirited' ways, Mark suggested that we stop at one child. I would say to him, "Only is lonely". I didn't want her to be lonely. I wanted her to have a sibling. Eventually, he conceded, and we had Madeline.

Madeline was born in 1999, is 20 years old and has graduated from university. When she was a baby, Madeline was the opposite of Lauren. Maddy was quiet, calm, almost docile. She did not have the intense spirit that her sister exhibited. In fact, Madeline's docile nature and lack of curiosity about her surroundings piqued our doctor's interest which led us down a road of assessments, therapies, specialists and medical labels. Parents take so much for granted with their children and assume their development will follow the usual pattern:

they will grow and have ready friends, work hard in school and graduate to possess all that life has to offer, just like their peers. While I will explore Madeline's diagnoses (cerebral palsy, autism, osteopenia, scoliosis, ADHD, and severe anxiety) in greater detail later, their initial impact left Mark and me with a sense of disbelief, uncertainty and loss. Somewhere in all of this, the connection that brought us together began to fray. We both loved our daughters fiercely and wanted what was best for each, and it would be unfair to say that it was parenting that became a wedge that drove us apart. There were too many shared medical appointments, concerned conversations and specialist meetings for that to be true. Whatever the reasons, they are not central to this story. Simply, a drift was upon us and we separated in 2006 when the girls were just seven and nine.

I think children of divorce work particularly hard to avoid that happening to their marriages. My parents' divorce was one of the reasons I did not get married until I was 27. I wanted to be sure that I wouldn't become a 'statistic'. But there are no guarantees in life, and the best laid plans can still go awry. The first few years after our divorce were tough. We were trying to navigate co-parenting while trying to be cordial with one another in an emotionally turbulent time. We did our best and became better at it as time went on. To say that the kids did not feel the effects would not be true. There is no way a child can come through divorce unscathed. We just did our best to minimize the scars.

In time, Mark met Tania and in 2010 they married. She has been an asset to Madeline's team of people. I am grateful for her. She has two children – Hayley and Oliver. Lauren and Madeline love them dearly and enjoy the moments that they get to spend together.

In 2018, I married Scott. As I mentioned, Scott and I have known each other since I was 23, when he was part of the team that hired me for my first teaching job. It had taken us many years to realize that our relationship could be richer than just a friendship. Anyone who is a single parent knows that trying to juggle kids and dating takes a lot of planning and a lot of energy. Sometimes, even the idea of dating can be exhausting – to the point of not even bothering to try. But Scott and I decided to make the leap from friendship to dating and we haven't looked back! As Adriene Mishler says, "Hope is a muscle", and I have always been a fan of keeping that muscle strong!

Scott and I are best friends and have seen each other through many ups and downs. He has known my children their whole lives and became involved as a bonus dad when they were in high school. Scott has two children of his own – Kieran and Claire. Kieran is 30, a graphic artist and the person responsible for the cover design of this book. He is a proud bonus brother to Lauren and Maddy. His laughter and easy-going nature add an element to our family dynamic that reminds us to live in the moment and not take life too seriously. Claire is 22 and goes to university in the city. We don't see her as often as we would like as she is busy with school and work. When she is not at school or work, she is travelling abroad so we appreciate the rare times that we all are able to come together.

The 10 of us are the inner circle of Maddy's village. Maddy is the glue that brings us together and holds us together. We are deeply interconnected.

I share this background information with you as it helps to know the timelines and characters in these stories before delving in. This collection of stories is not organized chronologically, it is organized around myths. Myths that we have encountered as Maddy's support system for the past 20 years.

I share the stories of our lives through the eyes of a parent and through this lens: *"Happiness is not something ready-made. It comes from your own actions"*. At every turn in my life – parents' divorce, career, my own marriage, having children, my own divorce, remarriage -- I keep this quote lodged in my brain, ready for quick access when I need it.

> *"I come to you humbly not to tell you what to do on your journey but to share with you what I have learned on mine."*
>
> *Wab Kinew*

Prologue

Pit. Pat.

Pit. Pat.

I am lying in bed listening to the rain as it begins to fall.

The tempo increases—pit, pat, pit, pat.

Now I am awake. I force myself to keep my eyes closed and think, *Lisa, don't look at the clock. Don't look at the clock.*

Too late. I look. It's 2:33 a.m. My mind is awake. The struggle is on between my thinking mind and my feeling body. My brain is engaged. The self-reflective questions start to fire.

Did I do my best yesterday? What can I do better today? What should I have learned that I can take with me into my future? Am I being the best version of myself?

The answers vary depending upon which lens through which I am looking at things -- that of parent, wife, friend, daughter, sister. I lay there a little longer, running through these questions, trying to find a path. I use my yoga breathing to calm my mind, hoping my body will follow suit. Eventually I fall asleep again and when

I awake, it's 5:30. I lay there until my husband gets up for his morning run. Before he heads out, we discuss our map of the day, and typically it revolves around Madeline.

Madeline is the amazing 20-year-old who lives with us. She is my biological daughter and my husband Scott's 'bonus' daughter, as he lovingly refers to her. While he is not her biological dad, he is fully involved in her parenting and support.

Now, you might be asking yourself, "Why would a 20-year-old require a particular type of parenting and support?"

The answer is that Madeline is a person with autism, a person with cerebral palsy, a person with anxiety, a person with ADHD, a person with osteopenia, a person with scoliosis and a person who requires daily support for some of these things. I believe every person has diverse abilities. Our differences are what make us individually unique and collectively diverse. 'Person with diverse abilities' is a term we use in our house when Madeline asks why her abilities (like walking) are not the same as everyone else's in the house. Not only does Maddy need support with her gait and walking, but she also has challenges comprehending the world around her. Diagnoses like Maddy's autism are sometimes thought of as "invisible", as anxiety or depression can seem to be, but if you know what to look for, there are visible cues.

Chapter 1

Myth: Your disabilities will shrink your horizons

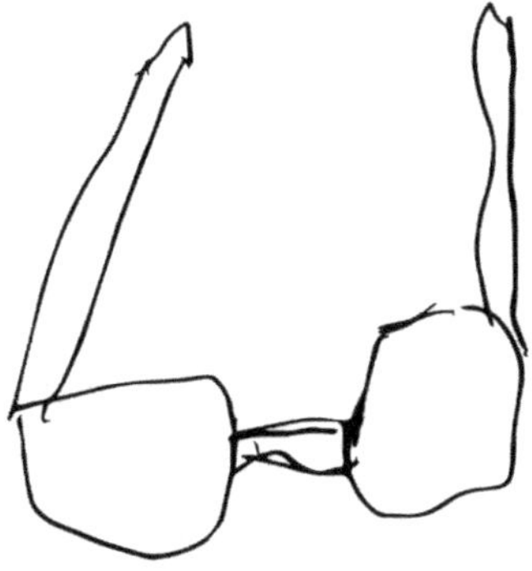

Although we did not receive a diagnosis of autism for Madeline until she was eight, there were definite indicators early on that she was wired differently than Lauren, our other daughter. In kindergarten, Maddy spent most of the first couple of months under the table, refusing to come out even when her lovely and kind teacher tirelessly tried to coax her with her favourite toys. When she did venture out, she struggled to interact appropriately with other kids and had a difficult time expressing herself clearly. Unlike most kids, she didn't seem terribly interested in other children. Thankfully, kindergarten was only half a day long, so school for Maddy was over at noon.

When we first enrolled Maddy in kindergarten, to help her transition to that setting, Mark took the first half of the school year off so one of us was always available to her. We were well aware that she was going to face challenges physically, emotionally and socially. Getting that time off was an ordeal in itself, but suffice it to say, our advocacy for Madeline made us resolute when her best interests were at stake, though we experienced many barriers along the way. We were never dissuaded by those barriers; in fact, they just made us better problem-solvers.

The types of challenges we encountered were myriad. For example, when it came to institutions like schools, typically the rules didn't fit the circumstance of our child (and this was often admitted). However, rules were rules and were stuck to. We fought the same battles for Maddy repeatedly and as time went on we discovered that once our reasoning was explained, logic usually prevailed. It was a great relief for me to have Mark guiding Maddy through each day during her first exposure to school life. It would have been a very different start for her if both he and I had been working full-time. When I think back on our journey, I honestly don't know how we did it. She just needed so much at that time.

Among the many challenges Maddy faced was wearing specific shoes that her orthotics fit into. As you can imagine, these shoes were never the ones with sparkles, light-up soles or anything remotely attractive. That's why some evenings when I came home from work, I would walk through the front door to discover a sparkly pair of little shoes pilfered from a classmate and neatly lined up under the bench. In Madeline's own way of communicating, by taking the shoes that had the most bling, she was telling us that she wished she too could have the exciting, pretty shoes. Each morning, we would pack the 'stolen' pair into Maddy's bag to be returned to their owner and put her own shoes on her feet. It broke my heart, but it was the way it had to be.

Playdates were a challenge with Madeline at that age. In kindergarten, she had not yet developed the ability to focus during social activity and could not grease the wheels of a relationship through the usual interactions of play and laughter. Instead, the initial excitement of a new child entering our home soon faded when the rambunctious play of a five-year-old was not reciprocated by Maddy. Mark ended up being a master organizer of the playdate, chatting to other parents on the playground and after class, and arranging social times at our home. He also became an integral part of the playdate, keeping things moving at a pace that kept the friend engaged. He liked to joke that he was a favourite of the six-and-under crowd and a master at the game 'pop-up-pirates', but this was to gloss over the sad fact that true friendships were not yet beginning for our daughter. I often prayed for just one good friend, one child that loved Madeline for who she was. My prayers were answered, but it was a long road before that person appeared and there were many tough years of isolation to slog through.

There is a saying in the world of autism: if you know one person with autism, you know one person with autism. The message is that autism presents very differently from person to person. In Maddy's case, she does not shy away from social situations. She loves to be in the mix and among people, which is not typical of many people on the spectrum. Where she *is* typical is with her rigid thinking and need for rules and routines.

Because of her need for structure, it was a huge effort to travel. I loved travelling but mapping out a 'cerebral-palsy-autism-friendly' vacation was challenging, to say the least. However, I was determined that my family would have the opportunity to travel, just like any other family and I have always been a stubborn advocate for my children so when Maddy finished elementary school (sixth grade), my sister and I decided to take her and her cousin Ben to Disneyland for four days.

Like most people, my sister had never been in close quarters with a child with autism and so this was an eye-opening experience for her, but one she lovingly embraced with energy and enthusiasm. From the flight, to the appropriate hotel room, to sleeping, to eating, to going on rides—everything had to be mapped out and all potential hazards and stressors anticipated. She was amazed at the planning and front-end loading that went into making each day a positive day.

I had learned that, for everyone to have a positive experience, consideration of Maddy's rigid thinking needed to be a top priority. One day at the 'Happiest Place on Earth' we were deciding which rides to go on. I knew the Matterhorn was not running that day. I also knew that it was best not to mention the word 'Matterhorn' or Maddy would fixate on it and all her attention and focus would be put onto that one thing, to the point where she would not be able to consider other options. However, I forgot to mention the 'unmentionable' word to my sister, and so she and my nephew quite innocently started talking about not being able to go on the Matterhorn that day. Well, that was it! After two hours of looping repeatedly around the topic, Maddy was finally able to consider a different ride -- and I was ready to hop on the next plane home! These looping conversations are typical of people with autism, but they can be exhausting for parents of kids with autism. One of the things I learned since that trip which I wish I'd had in my toolbelt of strategies then is that planning for Maddy is really planning for everyone else. Shelley Moore uses a bowling analogy to explain this strategy: if you aim toward the outside pins which are the most difficult to knock down, you are likely to hit a greater number of pins than by aiming toward the inside of the set. By planning for Maddy's needs, all our needs could be met.

In the end, the most rewarding moments of that trip were when my sister and I were seated around the pool and the kids were swimming. Disneyland, while wonderful, is not fun for a child with autism in the same way it's fun for other kids. At least when we sat around the pool, the kids were enjoying themselves in a contained environment. Also, it was then that I got to relax and was able to sit and chat with my sister without having to anticipate potential upsets. Today, when I think back on that trip, I am shocked at how well we rode the wave of exhaustion with humour and patience to ultimately have a very positive vacation.

In the summer of 2013 when Maddy was 14, Mark and Tania took Lauren and Maddy and their stepbrother and sister, Oliver and Hayley, on a vacation to Hawaii. They were not there 60 minutes when Lauren went down a waterslide at their hotel and broke her collarbone! It was not the best way to start a trip, but Lauren was a trooper and did her best to enjoy the holiday after her visit to the emergency ward. Maddy, however, could not let go of the fact that everyone in the group was doting on Lauren—making sure she was comfortable, asking her if she was okay, fetching things for her. It was difficult for Maddy to share the spotlight with her sister. Usually, it was Maddy who was doted upon. By the end of the trip, Maddy wished *she* had a broken collarbone just so she could have had the attention Lauren was having. Well, in a bizarre sequence of events, on the day their dad brought them home, Maddy went outside to play with the neighbour's child and as they were running around our front yard, Maddy tripped and landed on her shoulder. She immediately began screaming, "My shoulder, my shoulder!" as she lay face down in the dry, hard, brown grass crying uncontrollably. We didn't know how best to move her but eventually, Mark and I got her into the back of my SUV and I drove to the emergency room. After waiting for six hours, we finally got an X-ray—a broken collarbone! Maddy's wish had come true.

Helping one child with a broken collarbone get showered, changed and ready to go each day was daunting enough, but having to do that for *two* children almost pushed me right over the edge! There were nights I went to bed wondering if I had the energy to do it all over again the next day. *Just press play and repeat*, I told myself. Luckily it was summer, so we didn't have to get ready early for school each morning. Lauren, however, had a part-time job, so she had to take a few weeks off until her injury healed.

2015 was a busy year for us. Maddy was starting a program to help people with autism navigate the social world more smoothly. The Program for the Education and Enrichment of Relational Skills (PEERS) is a social skills program that teaches middle and high school students (grades seven to 12), with high-functioning autism or Asperger's Syndrome, how to make and keep friends. It is a 16-week program that works with both kids and their parents to help them learn social nuances. Maddy went to her class while Scott and I went to ours. Maddy learned new skills and had opportunities to practice with other kids while Scott and I learned the theory behind the skills and helped Maddy practice by doing homework with her each week. It was a long program, and Maddy gained many helpful skills, but it became obvious to us that no matter how hard she tried, there were just some things that were intuitively understood by others but were a struggle for Maddy to make sense of. You can teach a person to understand such things as personal space, or to wait for someone to answer a question before you ask the next one; however, subtle things, like reading facial cues or understanding when someone wants to get off the phone, are harder to teach, because intention needs to be *inferred*. Sometimes, people with autism are not good with inference. Scott and I truly believed Maddy could learn anything she set out to learn, but clearly some things would take longer and require more practice.

It wasn't until the year of the PEERS program – four years after Disneyland – that I could muster the energy to travel again with Maddy. Don't get me wrong, I loved showing her new parts of the world, and her eagerness to explore and take part in every opportunity at each destination were valued traits of a great travel partner, but the thought of planning out each day in advance and repeatedly saying no to many extravagant requests made even the idea of travelling daunting. The impetus for our next trip was that my dad had been given a free week at a new time-share condominium in Cancun. He gave it to Scott and me as the flight was too long for him. I was intrigued with the idea of going somewhere new, but I was also quite apprehensive about taking Maddy on such a long flight. With the layover included, the travel time was nine hours—a long time to be on the road with a routine-loving child with autism. However, I gathered my courage, took a few long, deep breaths, grabbed Scott by the arm and booked the trip. Lauren was unable to join us as my sister was taking her on a trip for her graduation at the same time.

I immediately had 'post-purchase regret' and started second-guessing the wisdom of taking a trip of this length. Scott reassured me that he was there to help and that we were in a self-contained resort so the potential for overwhelming choices (like those we'd had to make at Disneyland) was limited. I felt better and decided that, for better or worse, we were doing this.

The flight itself was uneventful. Maddy watched movies and read her book. She was in her glory at being able to watch unlimited movies because at home she only got one hour of screen time per day. We made it to our resort without too many bumps along the way but the challenges began even at that self-contained resort. Again, we were met with choices: the choice of two pools or the beach; the choices between six different restaurants; and, many choices of unlimited food and drink. Because we had never been to an 'all-inclusive' resort before, neither Scott nor I had anticipated this and so we knew immediately that we needed to map out a routine in order to be able to communicate quickly to Maddy what we were going to be doing, and when. If presented with too many options, she would become distressed.

We did some quick, on-the-spot problem-solving. In order to make our experience manageable and enjoyable, each night we worked with Maddy to map out our daily dining options for the following day. We couldn't just decide *for* Maddy. We wanted to include her in the decision-making because it was her trip as much as ours; however, with her, no decisions could be 'on the spot'. Maddy needed to know what was happening next or she got very anxious. Further, if we let Maddy decide completely on her own she would set herself into a tailspin and make no decision, so a group effort was required. Ultimately, her favourite restaurant became the Italian one where the server paid her all sorts of attention. She was a sixteen at this time and so she quickly became smitten with him and asked to eat dinner at that restaurant each night!

Our friends joke that there is always a story when Scott, Maddy and I go anywhere. They're right. And this is the 'time-share story'!

Upon arrival, we were informed that in order to use the 'free week' voucher, we had to attend a presentation about the time-share. It was expected that all adults would attend the session, which meant that Scott and I had to go, but what was Madeline going to do? We couldn't leave her alone at the resort while we attended a 90-minute session! She would have to come with us.

Thirty minutes before our scheduled session, we gave Maddy some specific instructions about expectations during the presentation. The short version was: JUST LISTEN. Our worry was that Madeline would be highly impressed with what we were seeing, and she would be all-in with whatever they were asking of us in terms of purchasing something we couldn't afford and didn't really want. And then the fixation and the looping would begin.

Well, we were right to be concerned. If you have ever attended a time-share presentation, you probably know that they rarely finish in the allotted 90 minutes. I had been to two of them and they usually lasted for two hours or more. At this session, the 90-minute presentation turned into *three* hours, because at every turn, Maddy said, "We should do this!" which prompted the presenter to declare, "Your family will make some wonderful memories at this resort." This went on and on. For every refusal Scott and I made, Maddy would make a positive comment that led us down the next 'pressure pitch' path until we went from 'ground-floor apartment and walk-out beach access' to 'fifth-floor penthouse with roof-top patio and 360 degree view of the bay'. At each new level of pressure, Maddy gave positive feedback, completely fixated on the dream they were trying to sell us. Thankfully, we held our ground and finished the three-hour presentation without owning a condo. However, Maddy was not impressed and it took some time to coax her out of it. Despite small incidents like these, the overall feeling leaving Cancun was one of success and peace, with many great memories. It had turned out to be the perfect vacation spot for her to read her book, drink virgin piña coladas on the swing, and snorkel in the ocean with Scott. She had a great time, with minimal meltdowns, which increased my confidence about travelling with her in the future.

Two years later, in 2017 when Maddy was finishing high school, I was invited to Orlando, Florida to present at an education conference. There were no time-shares involved in this trip and since Orlando just happened to be the home of Disneyworld, I thought I would be a terrible parent if I didn't find a way to include Madeline in the adventure. Lauren was writing her exams at university, so she was unable to join us. I was only going to be there for four days, so Scott and I managed to spring Maddy from school so she could come with us. Again, the flight was nine hours long, but I wasn't too concerned about it because she had already proven she could entertain herself on a lengthy flight. It went well and we all arrived in Florida intact and relatively non-frazzled.

The theme park itself was completely accessible for Maddy and her physical abilities. We even acquired a 'disability pass' that allowed us to go to the front of the lineups. We were wondering how Maddy would react to the sights and sounds of Disneyworld. It had been many years since that Disneyland trip, and she'd been overwhelmed by the place. And in Orlando it was not the noise, crowds, flashing lights or the lady calling in her southern accent, "Be polite, stay to the right," that bothered Maddy. Again, the most difficult part for Madeline was being presented with overwhelming choice: food, drinks, entertainment—it was all too much.

We understood right away, and using our Cancun experience as a guide, each night we worked with Maddy to map out the next day so we knew which rides we would visit, which characters we would see and which food we would eat. Even though most days at home we work on "flexible thinking" to help expand Madeline's rigid mindset, mapping was necessary for trips.

After our positive experiences with the Orlando trip and three years after visiting Cancun, we were ready to return to Mexico with Maddy. This time we tried the Pacific Coast of Mexico and booked a place in Puerto Vallarta. This trip was different from our other travels because it would not revolve exclusively around Maddy as our previous ones had. We were going as a group of seven, with other family members. I was so excited about this trip. Scott and I had never expanded our travel circle to include extended family members, as it had always seemed like such a huge undertaking to coordinate trips with more than four people. It was new territory for us, but we were up for it—sunscreen and sense of humour in tow!

Scott, Maddy, Lauren and I were traveling with Brenda (my sister), Ben (my nephew), and Kieran (my bonus son). Because the range of interests and abilities within the entire group was diverse, we prefaced the trip with the idea that it would be a 'lazy, sit by the pool, beach vacation'. We even went so far as to say that we were not booking any excursions, so if anyone wanted a trip filled with exciting activities, they might not want to sign on for this particular journey.

As it turned out, we were all on the same page and during our vacation we mostly just hung out by the pool, frolicked at the beach, played countless rounds of card games and plain chilled out. We did take one excursion into a town called Sayulita, which is famous for surfing. Lauren, Scott, Brenda, Ben and Kieran really wanted to surf but since surfing was not in Maddy's wheelhouse of sports, I needed to look at alternate activities for her.

What was available for her and her abilities? We could swim in the ocean, play in the sand, go for a walk or just sit in chairs and eat snacks. Maddy wanted to go swimming. As Sayulita is famous for surfing, you can imagine the size of both the waves and the crowds, but Maddy was fearless. I was always one for letting Maddy take the lead on making her own decisions, and since she chose swimming, I had to muster my courage and not let the waves or crowds scare me off. I said, "Okay. Let's do this."

As we walked toward the water, Maddy was stopped by a couple of kids who were digging in the sand. They asked her if she wanted to join. With her beautiful, beaming smile she said, "Yes!", and that's what she did. I was smiling too because if truth be told, I didn't like to swim, and was only doing it for Maddy. The way it turned out, she still got to make her own decision about her activity, and I got to stay out of the waves!

As I said earlier, we always come back from vacation with a story to tell and this was no exception. Our final night started with the fanciest dinner we had eaten at a beach restaurant. We each had a drink, an appetizer and an entrée. At 1 a.m. the barfing started. First it was my nephew, then my sister, then Kieran. At that point, Scott started to panic thinking it was the eggs Kieran had cooked for breakfast (as our fridge had broken down that morning and the eggs were suspect). Maddy was next on the "barf train". Maddy had not eaten eggs for breakfast so we crossed them off as the culprits. I was feeling fine until 7 a.m. when I started to kiss the porcelain. Scott was really panicking at that point because it was our travel day. At 8:30, Scott fell victim. Lauren escaped unscathed. Maddy had it the worst. She and Scott still looked a little green while we drove to the airport that afternoon. Scott was able to contain his nausea; Maddy was not. Just as we made it through security and were entering the duty-free shop, Maddy yelled, "Bag! I need a bag!" Lauren was smart and had a few in her purse because she anticipated something like that might happen. Like a major league baseball pitcher, she launched the bag at Maddy in nanoseconds, in time for it to catch her last bit of stomach contents.

Despite this incident, it reinforced that not only do we travel well together but we can manage and make the most of every situation that comes our way – even the situations that we couldn't entirely plan for!

Our 'disabilities' do not have the final decision for us on what we can do and where we can make our way in the world. They might mean that we need to approach situations differently or to be creative with problem-solving, but they don't mean there are roads we automatically can't go down. All people have diverse abilities that will require support in some way at some time in their lives. The purpose for using the term, 'people with diverse abilities' is to understand, learn and humanize; not to judge and dehumanize. I hope there comes a time when we no longer need to distinguish people by their abilities in order to understand and accept.

Embrace the potential of your diverse abilities and do not let anyone make you think there are limits on what you can achieve!

Chapter 2

Myth: Labels are always a bad thing

They say it takes a village to raise a child. For a child with diverse abilities, it takes a village of caring people who have courage, kindness, stamina, patience, perseverance and a sense of humour! Beyond Maddy's four parents, extended family and friends, it has taken people from all walks of life to teach, guide and support her. Have you heard the saying, 'If I didn't laugh, I would cry'? That is one of my many mantras. My family life with Maddy is a daily adventure of navigating speed bumps in unexpected places. We have the day-to-day problems that most people experience, such as cars that won't start and spilled coffee. But in our world, we add in issues such as an adult-size child melting down because of something they just don't want to face that day.

While being a person with diverse abilities can be exhausting, being the parent of a child with diverse abilities means I have to have enough energy for the both of us. I wear multiple hats: inclusion advocate, unity ambassador, guiding educator and constant caregiver are just some of them. Because I've seen Maddy excluded from many situations, I make it a point to see the world through the lens of *inclusion*. The natural progression of becoming an adult — going through school, getting a job, possibly getting married and maybe having a family — involves choices and options. For Maddy and other people with diverse abilities, those options aren't always a given because at times, the world judges them by what they can't do rather than by what they can. Maddy is determined to change this perspective and I wholeheartedly believe that she will.

Maddy's first firm diagnosis of developmental disability came when she was four years old, but a few years before that we were aware that some developmental turning points weren't being achieved. At her 18-month check-up, a locum for our regular doctor had noticed

Maddy's low muscle tone in her legs and that she had not yet met some significant physical development milestones. That launched us into our journey of ongoing medical assessments. We were referred to a pediatrician, the only one in our town of 65,000 at the time. He was carrying a very heavy caseload, so it took us six months to get in to see him, and once we did (when Maddy was two), he referred us to our local Infant Development Program (IDP).

Under the umbrella of the IDP, Maddy saw an occupational therapist, a physiotherapist, and a speech therapist. By the time Maddy was three, we had weekly appointments with all these therapists and her diagnosis was 'global developmental delay'.

When a doctor throws a label like that at me, I tend to break it down into its manageable parts. Global = far reaching. Developmental = going through natural childhood milestones. Delay = slower to reach 'normal'. So, for me, what I understood was that Madeline had challenges with her development that were not 'normal' and were far-reaching. The good news? No one said that she would not catch up. That was my lifeline. Little did I know that from that point on I would invest all my energy into helping Maddy reach her full potential.

One of Maddy's physiotherapists soon suggested that she be referred to Sunny Hill Health Centre for Children for an in-depth assessment, as she suspected Maddy might have cerebral palsy. The assessment she recommended (considered a pre-school screen) was only done when children were four or older, so although the referral went in before Maddy was four she was not allowed to be assessed until she was of age. I can be a relentless advocate, so when she turned four in June, I repeatedly phoned to make sure her name was in the queue. By mid-August, we had our appointment. The testing was a full, exhausting day where, for four hours, Maddy was put through a number of physical and cognitive assessments. During the lunch break, she played while Mark and I met with the doctors to hear about their findings, a meeting that lasted two hours. They confirmed many things we had suspected. They confirmed Maddy had spastic diplegia, which meant she had cerebral palsy (CP). CP had affected her lower extremities, explaining the low muscle tone the doctor had noticed when she was 18 months old. They also told us that CP could affect her speech, her hearing and the muscles of her face (she tended to have a drooling problem when she was little and as she got older, she didn't notice when food was smeared across her face).

The doctors tried to pace themselves as they fired information at us. They felt we could not possibly absorb it all in one sitting, and they were right. However, we took golden nuggets of information with us from that session, and one of them was to never pre-determine what Maddy could do. She would be able to do many things—just not at the same pace or in the same way that other children did. That became another mantra, and to this day we continue to reinforce the 'I can' mindset with her. I remember driving back from Vancouver that day feeling numb, looking in the rearview mirror and smiling at Maddy in her car seat, thinking two things: how do I protect this sweet little girl from the cruelties of the world and how do I learn everything I need to learn to give her the happiest life I can?

As parents learning about CP, at first we were overcome, trying to familiarize ourselves with the therapies involved to ensure that Maddy's life was filled with purpose, dignity, opportunity and joy, but fortunately we soon found that the community support and resources were excellent.

Our next challenge was to educate friends and family about how to support Maddy and how not see her as 'dis-abled' but as being a person with 'diverse abilities'. In some people's eyes, Maddy was one person before she got diagnosed and a different person *after* her diagnosis. One family member began to completely re-think how she related to Maddy. She loved Maddy but struggled to understand what they might be able to do together. Could they still go to the park? Bike riding? Running? Trampolining? Most of our family and friends were completely unfazed, however. They knew that CP was just a label and that she was the same old Maddy before and after the diagnosis.

After Maddy's diagnosis, as a family we began to see that there was a spectrum of acceptance as people processed the new information -- the 'labels'. First, they started by becoming more tolerant of differences as they put in the effort to understand them; next, they accepted diversity as a good thing; finally, when diversity became part of how they saw the world, inclusion followed.

My family fought hard for inclusion, but some situations were more easily won than others. One example was Maddy's attending a swim club. Maddy was a great swimmer, loved the water and could spend hours in it. But was she easy to coach? Not particularly, as she had a hard time focusing on what people asked of her and an even harder time visualizing what she was being asked to do. We registered Maddy for a competitive swim club but after a few practices, it became painfully obvious that Maddy was the 'odd one out' due to the skill level and competitiveness of the other swimmers. We did not want to subject Maddy to feeling like an outsider, so we politely quit and soon discovered Special Olympics. I loved the community and camaraderie of the Special Olympics organization and Maddy was in her glory with the gang at Special O (as she called it) so in retrospect, it was a necessary step of discomfort to get to something that was a better fit for her.

While I am not a fan of labels if it means the person will be treated poorly or if their options will be minimized, I see the value in labels when they allow access to funding and resources. For Maddy, a label of cerebral palsy meant she would receive physiotherapy (PT), occupational therapy (OT) and speech therapy (SLP) through the Infant Development Program until she was five years old. Once she started school, it was the responsibility of the school district to provide the OT and PT. Unfortunately, in our school district we had only three OT/PT people to support all our students. At the time of Maddy's diagnosis, speech and language therapy was done on a consultative basis, but no direct therapy was given to students with Maddy's needs (she was considered to be high-functioning with her cerebral palsy). So, when Maddy entered school, we entered the world of private therapies. Fortunately for us, we were transitioning to the Child Development Centre (CDC) in the Fraser Valley at that time. The CDC provided her with occupational and physio therapies, but speech therapy had to be secured privately. It was important for us to address her speech. Maddy was having a difficult time both expressing herself and understanding what others were saying and it was hard on all of us. We found an excellent speech therapist who specialized in children, and I took Maddy for weekly sessions. She really enjoyed going, which eliminated a lot of stress. We played games and our speech therapist used to ham it up which kept Maddy entertained. My greatest hope was that speech therapy would end the high-pitched squealing she used as her main mode of communication and that she could learn sign language or some other form of communication that did not blow our ear drums out! Happily, Maddy became able to communicate quite well due to this early intervention she received.

Though Maddy had a diagnosis of CP, once she entered elementary school, we noticed there was more going on than just physical challenges. Maddy was doing quirky things in the classroom and had a difficult time connecting with peers. Often, she made inappropriate vocalizations instead of using her words. Outwardly, other than her obvious challenges with balance and walking, Maddy appeared to be a typical kid, so it was perplexing. I am a teacher and I've taught students on the autism spectrum, but when it was my own child, it was difficult to see the forest for the trees. It wasn't until we were sitting in a school-based team meeting to work on Maddy's individual education plan for her cerebral palsy that the penny dropped for me. The goals we were setting for Maddy were about her physical challenges but should also have been about the social, academic and behavioural supports she required to be successful at school. I stopped the meeting and said, "I think we need to explore further what is going on with Maddy."

We got a referral from our family doctor for a private assessment and spent three days exploring Maddy's speech, fine motor skills, social behaviour and cognitive abilities.

On the last day of testing, Mark and I had an informal chat with the doctor. He didn't give us a diagnosis, but we suspected autism. We had taken her to that specialist to confirm our suspicion so that we could get funding for the supports we knew she needed. We hoped the specialist would assess *all* of Madeline, that this expert would dig deeper and get to the truth, but when he repeatedly mentioned her ability to maintain 'eye contact' with him during his sessions, we began to think he had taken a narrower view. The ability to maintain eye contact was perceived as non-autism-like behaviour. Then and now, Madeline presents a unique mix of traits and behaviours. She *looks* 'normal' so many people expect her to be able to do things in the same way and at the same pace that other people do. We started to understand that she had fooled the specialist. Alarmed, Mark and I spent many hours categorizing and detailing her behaviours, which included a lack of awareness of personal space, fixations on odour, sensitivity to noise, rhythmic and loud rocking at night . . . and the list went on. All of this was sent to the doctor before our final meeting, but when that day arrived, the doctor acknowledged a global developmental delay, and summed up her condition as 'quirky' rather than Autism Spectrum Disorder (ASD).

No label. No funding. We were on our own.

Fortunately, we had also signed up to participate in a joint research project undertaken by the University of British Columbia (UBC) and BC Children's Hospital (BCCH). The doctor at BCCH was investigating a potential genetic indicator for ASD. Madeline, Mark and I went for the testing and what we discovered was that while neither her dad nor I had any DNA markers (a marker, it was explained to us would be some chromosomal abnormality), Madeline, however, was missing the tip of chromosome 2. This potentially supported that doctor's working hypothesis that genetics might be associated. Given this discovery, the research physicians wanted to look further into Madeline's autism diagnosis. In their study, other occurrences of chromosome 2 abnormalities had been noted in patients with autism. Our doctor wanted a second opinion to see if this might be the case with Madeline. She referred us back to Sunny Hill and the results of this second ASD assessment concluded that Madeline was on the autism spectrum.

The meeting where we learned about the chromosomal abnormality was a watershed moment for all 3 of us and

Mark and I felt its immediate emotional impact. We had once been told by a different specialist that Maddy would fulfill all her hopes and dreams but that we would just have to 'keep our hands on the wheel' for a longer duration as she worked through what had earlier been described as a 'developmental delay'. But we quickly saw that this newest information might suggest some hard choices down the road. There was a 50% chance that Maddy could pass along the shortened chromosome 2 to her children. It was unknown. This unknown added to the sinking feeling in our guts. Maddy was not with us on this trip to BCCH so the ride home was pretty sombre. I think both of us were thinking of our little girl, who enthusiastically played with her stuffies and dolls, calling them her 'children'. Together they went on adventures that she assured us would occur with her own kids. I think up to that point, we all shared in her vision and looked forward to one day being part of this aspect of her life.

In retrospect, those early days of Maddy's diagnoses make me think of a GPS that gets constantly rerouted because of detours. When you think of your child's life, you have expectations of the route they will take, but when those paths get blocked, you must follow different routes. At that moment, we had to 'reroute' our version of Maddy's future. However, sometimes detours come with the most beautiful scenery. We learned to slow our pace, adjust our priorities, notice and appreciate the small things rather than frantically moving from one appointment to the next. We started to practice gratitude for what we did have and the things we could do as a family. Maddy's positive nature has never wavered. She lives fully, trusts completely and loves wholeheartedly. Her bravery, open heart and open mind have given us strength to embrace the journey of the present moment rather than getting too caught up in the future for which we had initially planned.

New label. Rerouted once again. Embrace the journey.

Even before that point, though, we'd known Maddy was exceptional in many ways.

Madeline had some physical characteristics that her sister did not display which had also been commented upon by previous physicians. The ends of her fingers did not give her hands the usual convex shape. Rather, they slanted from longer to shorter in a line - her index finger being the longest through to her pinky which was the shortest. As well, the knuckle of each finger was receded into the joint. At that point we had not been given any explanation about the cause of either of these things and truthfully, with everything else that was happening, it slipped our attention. Now we had learned that the genes associated with the second chromosome influenced many parts of the body, including fingers.

During an outing to the park when Maddy was three, she was hanging from the monkey bars and asked her dad to help her down. Now, at that point in her life, Madeline's diverse abilities were not always easy to pick out, even for a parent; after all, she had run around the park and hauled herself up onto the monkey bars, so why she could she not just get herself down like any other kid? We had no way of knowing then that the scoliosis that would later bend her back and tilt her pelvis was already a problem for her. So, suspended only 10 inches above the ground, when her dad told her, "Just jump. You can do it," she dropped to the pea gravel and on impact immediately began screaming. I returned home from an outing with a friend to find Maddy cradled on Mark's lap in the living room, ice bag on her leg. Mark had taken her to the clinic, where the doctor had manipulated Maddy's leg and ankle to assess the damage and said, "If it was broken, I couldn't do this. If it was broken, I couldn't push here. Nope, you don't need an X-ray, just ice it." Yet, there she was hours later, still unable to put weight on her leg. I insisted we take her for a second opinion, a pattern that would repeat for many years, as Madeline had an extremely high pain tolerance. Her dad took her to the hospital for an X-ray and they returned hours later with Madeline sporting her first cast.

It's funny how life can run parallel lines that intersect at just the right moment. Maddy was three when she broke her leg. It was also at this time that she was being seen by the physiotherapist through the child development centre. Once Maddy's leg was healed, the therapist worked to help Maddy regain mobility and quickly noticed that she had a very awkward way of landing when she jumped. The physiotherapist taught Maddy how to do the 'motorcycle landing'—knees bent and arms bent at her sides. The theory was that teaching her the motorcycle landing would prevent her from doing the straight leg landing, which is what she'd most likely done at the park when jumping from the monkey bars.

Over the course of the next few years, Maddy would have a total of five fractures—leg, toe, arm, wrist -- enough that both the doctors and my family were worried and wanted to explore a little further. What the doctors concluded was that Maddy had osteopenia (a precursor to osteoporosis) which meant that her bones were not terribly strong, so the wrong fall or the wrong landing could easily cause a fracture. Besides adding another label (albeit a helpful one as it added to our knowledge), it triggered a new level of worry when it came to Maddy's welfare. She had to manoeuvre daily life in a safe way, but she could not possibly know everything she might encounter, and I could not be with her 24/7 to guide her. Added to this was the fact that Maddy did not possess a healthy sense of fear. That led to a lot of stress for our family because, when we weren't with her, we had to ensure the people caring for her knew how to effectively monitor and guide her.

Perhaps I wasn't terribly trusting during that phase of her development, but it was torture for me to leave her with anyone other than her dad or my best friend. As you can imagine, this made my world very small and meant I did not have a lot of time to myself. I knew that was not good for me, or my family, and I tried to move beyond it. With time and some counselling—and Maddy's development—I was able to expand our circle, and my trust, a little more.

Maddy's cerebral palsy meant that she had yearly appointments at Children's Hospital in Vancouver. While at one of these appointments in 2013, the orthopedic surgeon noticed a curve in Maddy's spine. He measured it and informed us that Maddy had scoliosis which likely contributed to her wonky (Maddy's word) gait and to the balance issues she was experiencing.

The scoliosis diagnosis (another label that led us down another road of help for Maddy) meant we had to attend the Gait Lab at Sunny Hill hospital every couple of years. Our first visit was in 2017 and our next visit is set for later this year. Each visit is three hours long, during which time Maddy is hooked up to electrodes connected to a computer that measures the way her muscles fire, how quickly her muscles respond to her brain's signal and how her feet land once the commands are completed.

In one of our quiet phases in 2014 (without fractures, casts, tests or follow-ups), Maddy started complaining about her toe being sore. When I looked closer, I noticed that it was curving in on itself. The only time I had seen a toe like that was on my dear old auntie and we always just thought she had gnarly toes that one could do nothing about. What I discovered was that it was called a hammer toe, or mallet toe, and Maddy had one! Our doctor gave us a referral to an orthopedic surgeon. Because we lived in a small city, it took a while to get in to see him but after three months of waiting, we got called for our appointment. We immediately felt at ease with the doctor. He explained that he could straighten the toe, but that a straight toe would mean some limitations in what Maddy would be able to do after the surgery. Because the surgery required him to fuse the bones in her toe, she would not be able to go on her tiptoes, jump, or run. It wasn't hard to agree to that, because the toe was causing Maddy so much pain. Even giving up trampoline jumping was easy for Maddy; she just wanted the relief that surgery would bring.

As it happened, I had just started a new job in September 2014, before her surgery (which was set for mid-October). I worked for a generous and understanding district of people who gave me six weeks off so I could help Maddy with recovery and therapy after the surgery. Although the recovery and therapy were no walks in the park as her cerebral palsy added another layer to it all, we made it through. It surprised both Maddy and me that a toe took that much recovery! Maddy, as always, was a trooper. She was sensitive to bumps or movements with her new toe, and that alleviated my worry that she would injure it in some activity.

As Maddy got older, she became a little cynical when it came to doctors' diagnoses. When she was younger, she would listen and agree, but probably didn't understand the ramifications of each new label. Then she became a much more critical thinker, sometimes disagreeing with a diagnosis if she didn't like it. This was true of her Type 2 diabetes diagnosis in 2017. During a visit to our orthopedic surgeon at British Columbia Children's Hospital, he noticed Maddy had gained weight. He ordered blood work to rule out thyroid issues but implored us to make sure that she lost weight because excess pounds were hard on her back, hips and knees, which didn't help with the challenges she faced from CP. We had tried unsuccessfully for a couple of years prior to this appointment to help Maddy to lose weight. We were healthy eaters but Maddy had challenges with portion control and had a deep love of sugar, starches, sauces and dips! When the blood test results were in, Maddy received word from our family doctor that she had Type 2 diabetes. She refused to believe it. Mark also refused to believe it, which was music to her ears, but not a good thing. The problem with her not accepting a diabetes diagnosis was that she didn't change her lifestyle, which could have put her at risk for all sorts of secondary issues. Acknowledging the diagnosis would have added a helpful label to the situation. We battled this for a year until Scott finally said, "Why don't we try Weight Watchers?" He offered to sign up with her, support her and cheer her on. Maddy signed up, still unconvinced it was a good idea, but after the first meeting, she was all in. She loved the group meeting, the sharing and the camaraderie. Maddy had always appreciated being a part of a community and Weight Watchers was a community of people who were working on the same goal as she was. Within her first six weeks, she lost 10 pounds—true motivation to keep going.

There were a couple of bumps in the road with Maddy's weight loss journey . . . like the time she spent $20 on chocolate bars, cookies and sugary drinks and consumed them all in one sitting; or the time she went with a friend to Subway and she 'had' to eat a 12-inch meatball sub so her friend would not have to eat lunch alone. I believe that was a premeditated plan, as Maddy left her lunch at home that morning so she 'had to' borrow money and buy a 12-inch Subway meal that included a pop and two cookies! However, it resulted in a setback during her weekly weigh-in and she definitely did not like that feeling so she became even more motivated to stay on track to lose her last 25 pounds.

Maddy still attends the weekly Weight Watchers meetings where she 'holds court' and openly and honestly shares how her week has been. Maddy is quite a character and usually not a week goes by that she doesn't have a story to share that leaves the group in stitches and loving her. Within five months, she had reached her goal weight – beaming with pride when she received her gold charm for that achievement.

Interestingly, as the weight started coming off, her moods seemed to stabilize, and she developed a more agreeable disposition. That might not have been due to just the Weight Watchers lifestyle, but certainly the healthy eating, exercise, camaraderie, support network and sense of control she felt about setting and meeting a goal all had a very positive effect on her.

What we have learned about labels? They are not necessarily or inherently bad. In some cases, you may want to **embrace** your label. It can be like a superpower: use it for good, use it to help teach others, use it to make yourself stronger. Be in control of it; do not let it control you. Regardless of our diverse abilities, we should use 'people-first' language, such as 'a person with cerebral palsy' or a 'person with autism'. Using this language builds understanding, unity and community.

Myth: You won't need to worry about the same things parents of "normal" kids do

Some people seem to think those with diverse abilities carry on along a flat path impacting nothing and in turn bearing no impacts. That could not be further from the truth. My daughter brought her own unique aspects to daily living and merged them with the wide variety of typical human experiences.

One aspect of Madeline's distinct way of navigating through the world allowed her to be easily influenced by others. For example, when Maddy was five, she had a summer playdate with a friend she'd met at preschool and had known for a couple of years. She'd had a few get-togethers outside of school time with this girl and everything had gone well, so I had no reason to expect problems. At the start, Madeline and her friend were playing outside on the swing set, jumping on the trampoline and laying in the grass, until her friend asked if she could go in to use the bathroom. Immediately, Madeline needed to go to the bathroom as well. My first instinct was to tell Madeline to wait until her friend came out and then go, but her friend asked if Madeline could go inside with her because she was scared to go by herself. I gave it the thumbs-up and continued chatting with Madeline's friend's mom. After about five minutes, I started to wonder why they weren't done yet. I waited a couple more minutes and then I went to check on them. They were not in the bathroom. They were not even downstairs where they should have been. Instead, they had made their way to the upstairs bathroom and were plastering wet toilet paper on the stairs of Lauren's bunk bed.

"Maddy, what's going on?" I asked.

She told me her friend had suggested Lauren would like padded stairs because it would be soft on her feet when she walked up them to her bed. With no discretion about the wisdom of such things, Maddy blindly followed without thinking about consequences. It was a nasty mess to clean up. Why, oh why, had I not listened to my intuition?

A year later, when Madeline was six years old, we went on a family camping trip to Drumheller, Alberta— our first extended driving/camping trip. We thought we had prepared ourselves well. We had a mixed CD of the girls' favourite music to sing along to, lots of snacks in each of their packs and we were prepared to play every travel game you could think of, starting with 'I Spy'.

Things started well, though we had a few challenges along the way. During one pit stop at Wells Gray Park, Maddy took 30 minutes in the bathroom while a line-up gathered outside. Inside, Maddy seemed unfazed by the loud, frantic banging of people who needed to pee. I encouraged Maddy to wrap things up, to which she responded in a not-so-quiet voice, "No. I need to take my time. The other people can wait."

These words were not said with anger or defiance, but since she had a voice that carried, everyone heard her. Her words were said simply as she was unable to comprehend the needs of the others waiting. She'd be done when she was done, and what could be wrong with that? She had no extraneous emotions attached to her actions, but I was mortified. Had she shouted or been selfish, the others waiting in line might have felt sympathy for me, the poor mother fully in the fold of her daughter's defiance. But Maddy's calm tone and my refusal to get angry with her made it seem like I supported what was undoubtedly perceived as selfish behaviour. When we finally emerged into the narrow hallway and walked the line that now extended past the Doritos display racks, I felt pinned to those racks by the looks of desperate and unhappy faces with near-exploding bladders. Like the woman in the IKEA commercial, I wanted to yell to Mark, "Start the car! Start the car!" so we could make a quick getaway. Madeline, however, strolled out to the car for the next stop in the adventure, smiling and greeting people as she walked by, as if she was a queen! Some of the other mothers waiting in line gave me understanding looks, which eased the sting and made me remember that I was not alone in these parenting experiences. I was grateful for that.

We arrived in Drumheller, found our campsite and then let two excited little girls go exploring. Lauren was a reliable kid and asked if she could take Maddy to check things out while we set up camp. Madeline loved these opportunities; her sister was her rock, an unconditional support with an adventurous spirit. On this occasion, summertime heat was in full force and because the campsite was packed with families, tons of kids were running around. Soon, the two girls found a group of kids to play with just two campsites down from us. I was always a little anxious during these childhood 'meet-and-greets'. Would they accept Madeline? Would they 'get' her and allow her to be herself? Would she be safe and not get injured? Would she make good decisions amid the excitement of social situations?

We did not fret over Lauren; Lauren was an old soul who knew how to look after herself—and others. When she was born, our friends would always comment that she was a serious-looking baby. In retrospect, I feel that Lauren was meant to be Madeline's sister. She provided a lot of support to her sister and to the family in general and, in comparison to Madeline, received much less daily attention. We used to joke that she almost raised herself, but the truth is that we were blessed to have a daughter who has always made rational decisions, is thoughtful and caring, and took immediately to watching over her sister. Lauren instinctively knew she had a part to play in Madeline's 'village' of support. We did, however, try to minimize the times she 'watched over' Madeline, as Lauren was a kid herself and needed her childhood, too. We always tried to make sure that Lauren knew that her struggles, heartaches and triumphs were no less important than Maddy's. She was never expected to 'parent', just to jump in and play the role of 'big sister' when needed.

Things were going well, with the girls hanging out with the kids from the nearby campsites. A girl a little younger than Madeline, wearing a colourful summer dress, captured Maddy's attention. Things could, and did, go sideways quickly for Madeline when it came to social situations. Being unaware of how to navigate social nuances but wanting to be liked is a recipe for trouble for many people, but it is 10 times worse for kids with autism. They can be easy prey. As it turned out, that young girl's pretty dress and a nice smile didn't mean she was nice inside. Instead, she quickly figured out that Maddy would do her bidding no matter what and so this camping trip became the first time we ever saw Madeline push another child.

It was shocking. We never got the full story but ultimately, we determined that this girl was at odds with another in the group. Making Madeline her pawn, she told her to go over and push the other girl. Madeline did just that. Playtime came to an end. Maddy said the girl in the dress told her to do it -- that the girl said Maddy could be her friend if she did. Maddy wanted to be her friend.

It would not be the last time Madeline followed harmful directions at the hands of a manipulative person, but it marked a clear beginning for us as parents. We had a daughter so desperate to fit in to a relationship that she was willing to follow any suggestion for inclusion, belonging and 'friendship', even ones that were harmful to herself or others. Brene Brown explains the difference between belonging and fitting in like this:

"Belonging is being somewhere where you want to be, and (others) want you. Fitting in is being somewhere where you really want to be, but (others) don't care one way or the other."

When Maddy was in grade six she did something that most kids wouldn't have done, simply because she had no idea of potential danger. She was at the far corner of the school field with her 'friend', who dared her to eat a plant. The noon hour supervisor saw what was going on and brought them into the school. Luckily, I worked at the school so they brought Maddy directly to me. I asked her what she had done and why and all she would say was that she was playing with her friend and that they both ate the plant. Because no one knew what the plant was (it was growing through the fence from a neighbour's yard), the lunch monitor and her teacher called poison control. In a state of panic, they described the plant as best they could to the responder. She said we should just have the girls each drink a cup of milk. Luckily, it had been hot lunch day at school so there was some leftover milk readily available. At that moment, I was tightrope-walking the blurred line I lived between parent and teacher. Fearful for my daughter, I brought Maddy to the staff room where she consumed a small cup of milk. She kept it down. The noon hour supervisor did the same for Maddy's 'friend'. There appeared to be no need to induce vomiting. But, to be on the safe side, one of the teachers who had a spare block took the plant to the nursery to have its identity confirmed. To our relief, the plant was not poisonous but the incident certainly rocked everyone at the school that afternoon, and showed once again how Maddy could be easily influenced even as she was getting older.

Maddy's world closed in on her when she entered high school. Maddy never identified herself as a person with special needs in her early life. Up until her high school years, she saw herself the same as everybody else. She knew some things were frustrating and more difficult for her than they were for her sister, but other than that she didn't think she was 'needy'. As she got a little older, we talked about how there were some things she needed help with and how her brain worked differently than other people's brains. We also talked about how diversity was a good thing and that it made the world more interesting to have many types of people in it. It is my opinion that *all* people have diverse abilities but to use the language of 'special needs' that Maddy had been introduced to and was struggling to understand, we would run through everyone in our family and talk about how their needs might not be visible but they were just as impactful as visible disabilities. I told Maddy that I constantly worried about her, and that was *my* special need. As a child, I sometimes was referred to as a "worrywart". It was an identity I did not like and one that seemed focused on my deficits, not my strengths, but I explained that when a person worries, it means that they think deeply and are sensitive.

"Of course, the flipside to a special need," I explained to Madeline, "is that it comes with a superpower. My superpower is that I am sensitive which allows me to be empathetic toward others." We decided that Maddy's superpower was that she was open, welcoming and genuinely interested in other people. And then we agreed that while having a special need can be challenging, we would not want to be without our superpowers.

But in high school she realized that the label of 'special needs' meant 'limitations' instead of 'possibilities' to most people. After the first day of high school, Maddy came home and said, "What is the resource room and why am I there?" Under an outdated paradigm, she had been scheduled into the resource room and was being referred to as a 'resource kid'. Soon she started referring to herself as a 'resource kid' or a 'special needs kid' as well, and that broke my heart. At home, we never used the language of 'special needs' with Maddy. We used the phrase 'people with diverse abilities' when she needed clarification on something, because we wanted her to understand that it was about abilities, strengths and potential, not about needs and deficits. We explained that through life she would encounter many phrases – 'disability', 'special needs', 'handicapped', 'atypical', to describe her varying abilities but the only one she should respond to was that of 'person'. ALL people have needs. This is what makes us human and diverse. That's why we are ALL people with diverse abilities.

During her first year of high school, there was little to no blending of 'resource kids' with 'mainstream kids', nor was there any looking at Maddy's likes or interests when thinking about her potential and broadening her learning journey. She was simply streamed into the resource room because the labels of 'autism' and 'cerebral palsy' had preceded her and that's where the supports were for her. If the supports were in the resource room then naturally, that's where Maddy's program was. Although the "evolution of inclusion" is at the forefront of our education world in 2019 thanks to people like Shelley Moore, it was not then. At that time, we were dipping our toes in the pool of integration but still unsure about how to take the plunge into the deep end and immerse ourselves in inclusion. Honestly, we didn't know what we didn't know.

For Maddy, the lack of integration with "mainstream kids" sucked a lot of joy out of the whole idea of going to high school. Being put in the resource room baffled her, because she saw all people simply as *people*. Why should she be separated from the other students when they were peers and equals?

We fought hard for inclusion. We understood that equity did not mean 'same'. It meant access. Access to opportunities. Access to the supports that would allow Maddy to meet her potential. We were tireless advocates and luckily had people at the school who had the courage to jump into the ring with us and fight the good fight to change some of the structures and systems of the school so that it was more inclusive of ALL students. Thinking innovatively with the school-based team in Maddy's final two years, we were able to make changes happen regarding her course options that moved away from integration towards inclusion. It was an open-minded group that embraced the idea of change. As Bruce Beairsto says, "Change has to come from inside." Together we learned what would work better for all students – a change that continues to this day. During non-class time, however, Maddy and the other kids from the resource room (many of whom also struggled with social aptitude) tried blindly to make their way through high school without neurotypical peer role models to show them the ropes. Maddy's weak aptitude for social understanding meant that she often struggled with friendships.

In one case, while riding the school bus, she always sat with a boy who wanted to be her boyfriend. However, this boy was not particularly socially skilled either and so was being quite physical with her on the bus. For Maddy's own safety, the bus driver assigned her a different seat. What did Maddy do each afternoon when she got on the bus? She went directly to where the boy was sitting and sat beside him. At first, when she was asked to move, she would. But, as time went on, she became defiant and when the bus driver asked her to move, Maddy started giving excuses as to why it was okay for her to sit there. As you can imagine, this became a source of frustration for the bus driver.

She had a schedule to keep and couldn't start driving until Maddy was properly seated. Maddy got written up twice by the driver, and each write-up led to a one-day suspension from riding the bus. Maddy started to comply only when, after the second suspension, the bus driver told her she would lose her riding privileges totally if it happened again.

Boys have always been a magnet for Madeline. From the moment of her first kiss she was bitten by the 'love bug' and she's been searching for her true love ever since. As Maddy struggled with understanding how to build and maintain friendships, adding the layer of intimacy required to be in a relationship was even more challenging. It's hard to attract people from the big ocean when you are swimming in the side channels. Those in the big ocean just didn't understand and often found the different approaches Maddy displayed intimidating or even a little frightening. For example, in middle school, Maddy was smitten with one of the cute boys. Obsessed, when he and his friends passed in the hallway or waited for their bus after school, Maddy's gaze would linger for an uncomfortably long time. At that age, interested gazes are generally not returned with the same intensity. Instead, it made the boys scurry away.

She became mesmerized by and infatuated with every aspect of boys—the way they talked, walked, looked and acted. When she looked at a boy it was like she had a Star Trek tractor beam on them and she could not pull her gaze away. When we came to pick her up after school, she played a game I called 'hide-and-seek pick up'. Afternoon pick-up meant we were interrupting her boy tractor beam and so to combat us, she would pretend she didn't see us sitting in the car waiting for her. She would give a cursory glance our way, but not make eye contact and then look away. It was infuriating!

"Maddy, why didn't you come over to the car when you saw us?" we'd ask when we finally got her loaded up.

Her standard reply was, "I didn't see you until just now!"

Of course, this was absolutely not true! Every time we dropped her off in the morning at school, we would front-end load her about the after-school expectations. We tried to teach her that by not coming to the car immediately, she was infringing on other people's time. We talked with her about how being honest, direct and truthful about seeing us showed respect for our time. She would nod her head in agreement and pledge that she would ABSOLUTELY come over to the car once she saw us. Unfortunately, the behavior change we were hoping our lessons would result in was intermittent.

There would be moments when she would come straight to the car, but that was the exception rather than the rule. That continued through high school as well. The agreement was that she was to wait on the bench, look for us and then come over and get in the car when she saw us. It rarely worked that way. Most days, I had to get out of the vehicle, walk over to her and say, "Hi Maddy."

To which she would respond, "Oh, hi mom!"

It sounds kind of funny in retrospect, but at the time it was frustrating and time-consuming. By the time Maddy got to university, it appeared that our "respecting other people's time" lessons had taken effect. Now when we pick her up, she comes straight to the car, no longer letting her infatuations impose on our time.

Besides the dream of having a boyfriend, Maddy also dreamt of having a job. Since she was 15 years old, she had talked about working at the local movie theatre or being behind the counter at Tim Horton's. Being a supportive parent, for three years I drove her around to pick up applications and drop off resumes and for three years, though she had a few interviews, she was unsuccessful in getting a job. The silver lining was that, through her interview experiences, she got good at anticipating what questions might be asked. Finally, after interviews at Tim Horton's, A & W and our local public library, she had an on-the-spot interview at McDonald's and got hired immediately!

She came home with her support worker that afternoon in late June 2018, and announced, "I have some great news! I got a job at McDonalds!" I knew I should have been happy for her, but instead I was terrified. It was a wonderful opportunity for Maddy to go out into the big world, but how would she be treated? My 'go-to' emotion was to protect her vulnerability and her innocence. Many years before, I had worked at the same McDonald's and had a fabulous experience but the main reason my experience had been so great was because I had friends working there with me. Maddy did not know a single soul in that place but she was still completely excited to start her job. While I hid my own fear, I admired her bravery and wholehearted approach to life.

Ever the vigilant parent, I wrestled with the idea of informing her manager of Maddy's less-obvious challenges. I sought out the advice of a wise friend who had a daughter with autism about Maddy's age, who had already been working for couple of years.

"Do you think I should intervene and talk to the manager?" I asked. "I'm wondering if they need to know her strengths and stretches so as to best teach her the skills that she'll need to be successful in the job."

I expected my friend to say, "Stay out of it and let her be independent. Don't meddle," but she didn't. Instead she said, "Absolutely talk to the manager. That way, they will have all the knowledge they need to personalize the job for Maddy." What I learned from that conversation was that by providing knowledge to Maddy's employer, I was helping her to be independent and successful. Without sharing Maddy's story, there may have been a whole lot of frustration based on expectations that Maddy wouldn't have immediately been able to meet in the same way that other employees would have.

Although I was not ready for Maddy to have a job and I didn't think she had enough people skills yet to take it on, her job turned out to be a great way for her to grow her skills and develop her independence. Sometimes opportunities present themselves before we think we have the necessary skills to take them on. However, it can often be through those opportunities that skills develop. (This I learned from Norman Kunc and Emma Van der Klift). Working built her confidence and made her more willing to try new things. I understand now that my fears were because I saw Maddy through the eyes of a parent. The manager at McDonald's saw Maddy through the eyes of an employer focused on running a team.

Maddy's approach to new experiences has been a fine balance of optimism and trepidation.

After she'd been working at McDonald's for a while, Madeline applied for a job at a local restaurant and got called for an interview. What made that job more attractive than her McDonald's job was that it was within walking and biking distance, so she could get there and home on her own, another step on the road to independence. Because Maddy really wanted that job, the stakes felt high. Before her interview, she endlessly stressed about what to wear, how to do her hair, etc. Now, I know everyone does that before an interview, but what made Maddy's preparation for an interview more involved were the questions that were unique to her: "Should I wear my big leg brace?" "Should I tell them I have cerebral palsy?" "Will they know I have autism?" "Will they hire me if they know I am a person with diverse abilities?"

Of course, the answers to these questions *should* be a resounding, "Yes, yes, yes and yes." It should have made no difference if her brace was on or off, big or small. It should have made no difference if she had CP or was on the autism spectrum. If she could do the job, what was important was that Madeline be accepted for herself and her skills. Basically, what she was asking was, "Do

I show them what they want to see? Or do I show them the real me?"

It gave me a better understanding of how people felt when they faced possible discrimination for cultural differences. It took me back to a conversation I had had with a friend of mine about cultural diversity and the struggle to be seen for who you are – learning that differences help us to understand each other. Maddy wore her brace, told them about her diverse abilities and got the job!

As part of Maddy's journey toward independence, one step was helping her develop the skills to get to school on her own without one of us driving her. There were a variety of options to try and the first was the handy-DART bus service. I clearly remember the day we first tried that. Maddy had never gotten herself up, made breakfast, packed her bag, got her shoes on, cleaned up and headed out the door on her own before. Of course, we'd provided opportunities for her to practice, but we'd always been available to monitor her and keep her on task if she got distracted. We wanted to transition her to independence, but we'd never really released ourselves to do that, nor trusted her to be able to take this step on her own. But it was becoming a matter of necessity. She was a young adult and had to go to school and we were still in the middle of our working lives. We couldn't be with her all the time. The day she had her first "fully-independent morning" was at the beginning of her time at university.

We'd arranged for the handy-DART to pick her up after we'd left for work, but because Maddy didn't understand the passage of time or the idea that other people's time was important, she was not ready when the handy-DART arrived. The driver waited in the driveway for 10 minutes before coming to the door to see what was up. Maddy said she just had to get her coat and shoes on and asked that he wait for her. He waited another 10 minutes and still she did not come outside. He knocked on the door again to find out she had been distracted by the dog. By the time they departed from our house, the driver had waited 30 minutes. He was a very kind man. The handy-DART was not supposed to wait for clients. The service gave a range of time to clients for pick up and drop off and people expected it to arrive and depart within that range. Riders were supposed to be ready to hop on the bus when it got there. By making the bus wait for 30 minutes, Maddy inconvenienced a whole lot of people.

The handy-DART didn't work too well for Maddy, so next we tried using a taxi service.

Given Maddy's sense of time/timing, you can imagine how using a taxi went. A major difference between the handy-DART and the taxi was that the handy-DART was a free service. The taxi was not. A taxi driver sitting waiting for Maddy was not too fussed because he just kept charging for every minute. So, while taxis helped us get Maddy to school, they cost us too much money!

What we have learned about dealing with issues as children with diverse abilities grow? We've learned that the path for them shares a lot of the same bumps as "normal" kids, with often unique aspects layered on. **All** kids are going to come face-to-face with issues, but just not in the same way or at the same time. We've learned that some people will try to lead you into their world of 'normal', but it's important to **embrace** *your* 'normal'. You get to decide what your normal is. Don't try to live to someone else's definition of normal. Conformity inhibits identity and personality. Conformity reduces diversity.

Chapter 4

Myth: Typical developmental stages do not apply

Without a doubt, Madeline went through the various developmental stages the rest of us did as children/young adults. The only difference for her was the pace at which she progressed. She sometimes got 'stuck' in one stage for a long time. When she was a teenager, she was stuck for a while in a stage of defiance and making poor decisions. That's not an uncommon stage for teens but Maddy's additional struggle with appropriate behavior and good judgment compounded her actions, causing us not only frustration but also sometimes outright fear.

As is common with many teens, Maddy had a need to be included and a need above and beyond anything else to have friends. This need for friends caused her to make decisions that were not always healthy or well thought-out. She had enrolled in the TASK (Training in Attitude, Skills and Knowledge for the Workplace) program at the university. The program provided workplace experiences for people with diverse abilities. TASK was particularly stressful for Maddy not because of the academic piece but because of daily social drama and so we told her that if she ever needed to take a mental health day, to let us know and then together we would make arrangements for that day.

Well, unbeknownst to us, that day came in mid-October and it was not the planned event we'd hoped for. I dropped Maddy off at the usual spot in the morning so she could meet up with a friend. From there, the two of them were to walk to the university campus, which was not too far from our house. From how things looked to me when I dropped her off, it was a typical day. The girls met up and I drove away assuming they were going to make their way to the university. My assumption that all was well carried me through my workday until after lunch. Checking my email, I found one from her teacher. We kept in regular communication due to Maddy's stress about the social elements of school. She was fabulous at keeping in touch with me and at the end of her email, she signed off with, "I hope all is well with Maddy today. We missed her in class."

I didn't immediately panic, as Maddy had been asserting her independence through occasional acts of pushing boundaries. Skipping school was a new one among those acts, but I decided not to panic until I had the pertinent information. After calling Scott and Mark, both of whom said they had not heard from her, I called home. I knew if Maddy was there, she would pick up the phone. No answer.

At that point fear kicked in and I decided I needed to leave work and begin searching. I had never experienced a situation like that before but knew that as soon as I put the word out about Maddy's disappearance, it would send a ripple effect through our circle of family and friends and all hands would be on deck. So first I had to make sure it was worth mobilizing the troops.

Something in my parental 'Spidey senses' told me that I would find her near food. I headed toward the village near our house where there was a multitude of restaurants, coffee houses and grocery stores. En route, I neared our neighbourhood McDonald's. I slowed down as I approached the traffic light and, as I looked out my window at the seating inside McDonald's, I spotted Maddy having a grand old chin wag with her friend. Luckily, the parking stall directly facing where she was seated was empty, so I slowly pulled up and made a lot of movement to catch her attention. She was so immersed in her conversation and talking with such animation, that when I came directly up to the window and tapped on it with my finger she didn't even notice. I was trying to be discreet, to be heard but not overly obvious. I didn't want to publicly shame her, but I wanted her to come outside to talk with me. As the volume of my tapping increased, both she and her friend turned around. Her friend immediately panicked, got up, started to cry and walked outside to see me. Not Maddy, though. She was far more reluctant. When she finally came outside to join her friend, Maddy asked me why I was there and became indignant that I was infringing on her 'day of relaxation'.

While I had been driving to find Maddy, I had been talking with Mark on my car's hands-free system. As I pulled up to McDonald's, I'd told him that I'd found her and kept him on the line. When Maddy came outside and gave me a hard time about ruining her day, her dad started talking to her over Bluetooth. Maddy stopped in her tracks, wondering where her dad was! It was a moment of comic relief in an otherwise tremendously stressful situation.

Maddy had not only got herself to McDonald's, but she'd brought along our dog Oreo (precariously balanced in the basket on her bike). I had to figure out how to get both Maddy and the dog home safely so I told her I would take the dog but that she was to ride her bike back home. The dog hopped in with me; Maddy and her friend rode their bikes to their respective homes. I waited for her outside our house. When she finally arrived (part of me nervously thought she might have decided to have another 'adventure' before coming home), I explained that I wanted to discuss the day's sequence of events. It didn't go well. She kept insisting it was her day to have and that I should not have interrupted it. I felt like I was pounding my head against a wall trying to get her to see how disrespectful, inconsiderate and thoughtless she had been. All she could see was that I had negatively impacted her day by fetching her before she wanted it to be over. The ironic twist in all of this was that we had to draw our debate to a close because Maddy had to get ready for me to take her to work … at McDonald's!

When I picked Maddy up from work that evening we debriefed the day's events on our drive home (when we were both calm). Without the intense emotion that the situation brought earlier in the day, we role-played each other's scripts. Through this, she was better able to understand how shocked I was to receive the email from her teacher and how panicked I must have felt as I left work not knowing where she was or if I would find her. Through our role-play I learned that she just needed a day to be a care-free teenager – away from the stress of university.

The stage of defiance wasn't limited to just that one incident. Maddy had an unusual trait which was to mimic people, especially if she was impressed by that person and wanted to start or maintain a friendship. Our community of people with diverse abilities has been, for the most part, a great place for Maddy to make some good friends and generally she's felt welcomed and had people to do things with. But the mimicking thing could present problems. For example, Maddy's friend joined Special O swim club with her partway through the season. Up to that point, Maddy had been working her hardest at getting stronger and learning more intricate techniques for her swimming strokes, becoming a very strong swimmer and meeting her potential each week. One day, we picked Maddy's friend up on our way to swimming and as soon as she got in the car, I could tell something was up. Her mood was quieter, and her demeanour was more reserved. She said that she was very tired. Immediately, Maddy said she was tired too. At that point, I should have listened to my intuition, turned the car around, dropped her friend off and drove home to put my feet up and read my book. But I didn't listen to that little voice in my head and instead we continued to the swimming pool.

Maddy was at that point imitating her friend like a circus mime. Her friend said she was tired, Maddy said she was tired. Her friend said she was going to take it easy at swimming, Maddy said she was going to take it easy at swimming. I got both girls ready and out onto the pool deck. I told them to swim their best, get a good workout and be proud of themselves. Then I went up to the observation deck to do some work of my own and to watch them. I soon realized that I hadn't seen either of them swim past me in a while. When I looked up, Maddy was at the end of her lane talking with one of the coaches and her friend was on the pool deck chatting with a different coach. My blood started to boil. I knew Maddy was in mimic mode again. It had been 45 minutes since swim practice started and I had only seen Maddy glide down the lane four times!

I motioned to her to get swimming and she looked back at me and shook her head, 'no'. Man, I felt like one of those cartoon characters with steam coming out of its ears! I said to her, "Get swimming!" and again she shook her head in refusal.

Finally, she swam a length but by then I was so frustrated, I walked down to the shallow end so she could both see and hear me better. I said to her, "Take your practice seriously. Don't waste your coaches' time. If you are not going to swim, we should go!"

She yelled at me, "I am not leaving! I want to swim!"

In my sternest voice, I replied, "You had your chance and you chose to chat instead of swim. We are leaving! The coaches need to focus on the swimmers who are swimming!"

Slowly and purposefully, she swam back to the deep end. I walked down to the pool deck and waited for her to get out and come to me. Her friend came over immediately and profusely apologized for not swimming. The coach came over. I explained that there was no excuse for Maddy not swimming and that in future, she should not swim in the same lane as her friend to keep the mimicking at a minimum.

Eventually, Maddy strolled up. I told her it was time to get into the change room. We were leaving and she needed to get a move on. So, there I was trying to get both girls out of the change room and into the car so the night could be over. Maddy was being obstinate, her friend was apologizing and all I wanted to do was go to bed! On our way home, once I was calm, we talked about the learning that came out of that experience. What did she learn? Well, she learned that our friends can feel one way and we can feel another way and that is okay. As well, she learned that it is important to listen to how we feel. If she truly didn't feel up to swimming and was not going to participate and do her best, then maybe the best idea would be to take a pass and get back to it the following week.

That same year, Maddy and her friend were having dinner at our house early one evening before Scott had to take them to swimming practice. Everything was ready for a spaghetti dinner: the pasta was cooked, the sauce was warmed, there was grated cheese to be put on top, and the milk was chilling in the fridge. Scott was outside helping a neighbour. The girls started eating so they wouldn't be late for swimming. However, somewhere in the middle of dinner, Maddy thought it would be hilarious if she fed our dog, Oreo, some spaghetti. Oreo kept eating spaghetti, Maddy didn't try to stop him, and ultimately, what went down came back up; the dog vomited all over our white carpet. When Scott got back inside, he was only able to do a cursory clean-up before swim practice, so Oreo's treasure was still there when I got home. I had to go at it with the steam cleaner—not what I wanted to do after a long day at work. Spaghetti barf on a white carpet is a stubborn stain. To this day, if you look closely, you can still see a faint orange glimmer, a constant reminder of the Maddy's unfortunate choice that day, Oreo's responses and the limits of our steam cleaner!

If we thought Maddy had a difficult time discerning appropriate behavior for her dog, it was nothing compared to what was awaiting us when boys began to show interest in her. It was then that her vulnerability *really* became a huge concern for us.

In Maddy's 'gap year' (she had finished high school but was taking courses part-time back at high school), we got Maddy a cell phone. Our rationale for the phone was that we were working on her independence by slowly giving her more opportunities to do things on her own. She was taking courses at high school for half the day and then coming home on her own to take care of the dog for a couple of hours before we got home from work. For us, the cell phone was for safety. She was to text me when she got home from school and then text me again when she got home from taking the dog for a walk.

In the beginning, she used the cell phone simply for communicating with her family—she texted Scott and me daily, she texted her sister daily as well and she called her dad every few days. Slowly, Maddy learned that the cell phone was a two-way device; not only did it allow her to send messages out, but if she gave her cell number to people, she would receive messages from others. This was very intriguing to Maddy. She began handing her number out indiscriminately to people that were not in her friends and family circle. As you can imagine, that posed many new challenges.

At first, we framed the phone to her as an object of privilege, making it clear she needed to demonstrate to us that she was responsible enough to keep this privilege. But she became obsessed with her phone and started getting into texting conversations with boys who were too old for her, who were sharing too much and who were leading her down the wrong path. We had to intervene. We took the phone and checked her calls and messages. We found that she had also discovered how to access her Facebook page via her phone, so she was receiving up to 30 friend requests a day! As time went on, she started to lose interest in her phone, and we implemented a new safety plan using our house phone. We realized that the cell phone was not a necessity and that it had caused more grief than it was worth. From then on, she used it only under our guidance so that we could ensure she was interacting appropriately with her contacts.

The great thing about having two very different children is that they trained us and provided contrast and wisdom in different ways. Lauren often reminded me that Maddy could do more for herself than I sometimes gave her opportunity to do and that helped me to let go a little. However, there were some areas of Maddy's development where I couldn't let go of concern, and yet no matter how much guidance I tried to provide, her biology overruled. Ultimately, I was raising a young adult who had the same urges as everyone else, but less of the judgment.

Maddy's eye for the boys meant that she was vulnerable and willing to accept attention no matter *who* it came from. At bowling club when Maddy was 19, she would hang out with the boys, get distracted by them and forget to bowl! She would hug each of them when they greeted her, and each would tell her he was her boyfriend.

Around that same time, she went looking for love in all the wrong places yet again. She was playing a game on her iPad while visiting her dad and a pop-up ad for an 'angel who can find you love' came up. Well, Maddy was in, hook, line and sinker! Long story short, she gave

ALL her personal information to this website and then got an email within a few short minutes from 'William' telling her that he was her angel and would guide her through her journey to love.

Knowing Maddy's vulnerability when using social media, I was set up as the gatekeeper for her email address and her iPad so when Mark let me know that there was an email about to arrive from 'William', I intercepted it and immediately terminated the communication. Once again, we had a conversation with Maddy about online safety, trusting others with your personal information and learning to discriminate between people who were well-meaning and those who were not.

Also, when Maddy was 19 she was waiting for us to pick her up after her first day at university. She had somehow managed to meet a boy who ended up being a source of drama and distraction for the entire first term of school. This 'boy' was actually quite a bit older than Maddy and was also a person with diverse abilities. He was looking into university programs for himself. Maddy started to chat with "Dan". By the time we got home from school, he had texted her (yes, she gave him all her information) *eleven* times. The texts ranged from "Hi," to "You are cute," to "I want to marry you in two years." Needless to say, this panicked Scott and me, and propelled us into a long conversation with Maddy that evening on a plethora of topics ranging from personal safety to appropriate interactions to using common sense. I thought back to a conversation with the doctors at Sunny Hill when Maddy was first diagnosed with autism. They said Maddy would have a hard time navigating the social world, that nuances would most likely escape her and that she would probably learn social skills through the school of hard knocks. Their words certainly rang true in this situation, but it didn't make it any easier to endure as a parent.

The "boy drama" carried on for the whole first term and caused a lot of stress for Scott, Mark, Tania and me. Not only did we have to ensure that the communication didn't cross any major boundaries and that Maddy didn't get into the situation any more deeply, it also ended up causing a rift between her and "Debbie", a slightly older friend at university. The rift developed because both girls were "interested" in Dan, and it devolved into an imaginary lover's triangle (imaginary because Dan never even went to the same campus as they did and Maddy never saw him again after their initial meeting on the first day of school). After several weeks of this and many conversations with her fantastically supportive instructors, Maddy was still fortunately "on track" at school. Together we agreed that her social interactions with Debbie should be limited so that she could focus her energy on her learning. The boy drama mercifully receded into the background.

Just a few months before she entered the work force, Maddy had her first boyfriend. Maddy was over the moon with their relationship. All she wanted was a boyfriend—even though they were as different as night and day. If they had been on Match.com, the two of them would not have crossed paths. "Jake" was a person with autism, like Maddy. He was very sweet, gentle and kind, but he and Maddy did not have a lot of common interests. However, Maddy was so excited to have a boyfriend that she was willing to overlook the fact that he did not reciprocate her feelings. As a parent, it was hard to watch but we and Jake's parents let it play out for a couple of months because we wanted to give them the opportunity to 'try on' a relationship. We helped to plan and support activities for them to share as a couple. As the relationship went on, it became harder and harder to find common activities for them. Jake liked video games, Maddy liked going for walks. Jake liked listening to music, Maddy liked watching movies. Jake liked being on his own, Maddy preferred being around people. Jake preferred cats, Maddy preferred dogs. In the end, Jake's mom explained to me that although Jake liked hanging out with Maddy as a friend he did not want it to be a girlfriend/dating thing and so it couldn't continue.

Maddy was crushed. It was heartbreaking. Mark, Tania, Scott and I sat down with her to try to console her about her first break-up and encouraged her to ask questions. While it was deeply upsetting, it was one more experience to expand her world. All that was left was to give her a big hug and time to heal. It was a reminder for us that Maddy just didn't yet understand all the nuances of the dating world. It was also a reminder that her access to the world was only as big as we made it for her. We often asked ourselves, "If this was Lauren at 19, what would she be doing?" Usually, the answer was, "Whatever she wanted." By 19, Lauren was living away from home, attending university, taking care of herself and driving wherever she needed to go. Lauren was an amazingly well-adjusted 19-year-old and, of course, her approach to the world, and the world's approach to her, was completely different than it was for Maddy.

What have we learned about developmental stages? Expect that the "typical" stages will be part of our lives, and that no one is immune from their effects. **Embrace** them as they come. They will come in their own time and in their own way, and they will take their own time once they get here!

Chapter 5

Myth: There is a limit to what a person can learn

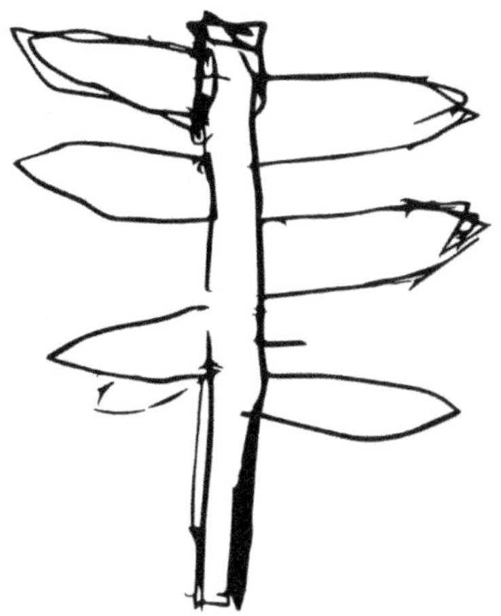

People with diverse abilities, particularly children and young adults, sometimes have very little actual control over their lives. Often, other people are organizing, scheduling, problem-solving and even *thinking* for them. This was definitely a spiral we found ourselves in with Maddy. When she was younger, it was so much easier to do 'for' her rather than do 'with' or have her do things 'by' herself because it took her four times as long as us to get anything done! Typically, we didn't have four times the time, so we did a lot for her. That of course, did not help guide her toward independence; in fact, we unwittingly made her more dependent.

For as long as I live, there is one conversation that will remain burned into my memory. It was a conversation we had at a school-based team meeting when Maddy was in grade three (she was eight years old). Sitting around the table was Maddy's support crew: Mark, me, and members from the school and district. Now, the person from our district (I will call him Taylor) was not at Maddy's school full-time. The school Maddy attended was a small school, and so, based on that, Taylor was only scheduled to be there one day a week. He spent most of that one day doing paperwork and as far as I knew he had very little face time with the students on his caseload. Because of this, he knew Maddy through paperwork, but not as a person.

Everyone had finished sharing their experiences with Maddy and we were getting to the part of the meeting where we started to problem-solve and develop an action plan when Taylor looked at Mark and me and said coldly, "You know, Maddy will never learn beyond the level of a fourth-grader. In fact, she will probably reach her full potential by the time she has finished grade four."

Everyone at the table gasped. I could see Mark preparing to go all 'Papa Bear' and react in anger. I understood his urge. *All* parents want the best for their children, and parents of children with diverse abilities particularly want positive reassurance that their 'village' supports them. For an educator in our system to be so cold and negative was not inspiring and had not been our experience thus far. However, it made me understand very, very clearly that we would have to advocate for Maddy all her life, because often others would not.

What Taylor said was dead wrong. However, on these things we *could* agree with him:

- Her elementary school years were trying and her transition to intermediate grades was hard.
- She still had all her social awkwardness and her physical limitations were increasing.
- She was becoming aware of her differences in a way she hadn't been when she was younger.
- Children were becoming critical of her and she was becoming more isolated.

But what Taylor *didn't* know about Maddy was that, despite all of that, she remained a positive soul. In each of our homes, we parents saw a girl who was curious, creative, interested in a variety of things and always welcoming to whomever she met, despite the increasing knocks of school life. How dared Taylor, who didn't even know our daughter, tell us that her glass ceiling would soon be reached? It was dismissive. It was final. Her dad and I did not believe him and were angered by his attitude.

Now I generally strove to be a calm and patient person. I did yoga every day. I worked to see the best in each person and each situation. But in this situation, with this person, I did not feel calm *or* patient. In fact, I had a visceral response to his words. I immediately felt as if I was having an out-of-body experience. Inside I thought, *he cannot be talking about my kid. My kid will reach whatever goal she sets for herself.*

Outwardly, my thoughts showed in the form of tears streaming down my face. I was incensed that he was speaking these words about my daughter; however, I knew that this was a pivotal moment in Madeline's education, and we needed to stake our ground on her behalf. I broke the silence by asking, "What makes you say that?"

Taylor's response was, "Well, I have worked with lots of 'these kids' and they all end up hitting the ceiling at a grade four level."

Again, I had the visceral response to his dehumanizing comment, but this time, I was calmer and more in control of my emotions, and I stated clearly, "Maddy is not 'these kids'. She has always surprised us with what she can do, and I would bet that she will continue to surprise us. It is not our job to put a limit on how much she can learn or how far she will go. Instead, it is up to us to guide her and *support* her as far as she *can* go!"

At that point, the principal called an end to the meeting as it was not going in a positive direction and in that 45-minute session we were not going to change Taylor's view of people with diverse abilities.

I have often reflected upon his words and that meeting. What would he say if he could see Madeline now? She is a lovely, personable and positive young lady, welcoming and open; her mantra of 'never give up and always believe' powers her along. In the summer of 2018, she completed her grade 12 equivalency and in 2019 she graduated from a university program designed to help her be employed and live an independent life. She got a job. Where would we be if we had merely accepted Taylor's judgment and opinion of her when she was in grade three? Although Taylor only worked in our school district temporarily, my hope for him is much like how we view seat belts in cars. When I was a little kid, we used to hop into the back seat of my dad's car and roll or slide around when he took the corner because there were no seatbelts to hold us in place. It was just the way things were done in the '70s. Would we do that now? Of course not! And why not? Because we know better. My hope is the same for Taylor. After all of the meetings and learning opportunities available to him over the last 12 or so years, I hope he has embraced those opportunities and now knows better how to have conversations with parents of children with diverse abilities. I try not to take things personally and I assume that people are doing their best with the knowledge they have at any given time. Like Maya Angelou said, "Do the best you can do until you know better. Then when you know better, do better".

As a family, we always knew that Maddy could learn what she set her mind to. One of the things we dedicated some time to was teaching Maddy how to be both a gracious loser *and* a gracious winner at board games; it's still a work in progress! We started by playing simple games that she could understand and completely participate in. Two of her favourites were Princess Monopoly and Trouble. As the games were ending, she would start to get anxious and angrily asking, "I'm not losing, am I?"

In the beginning, we would buffer her from losing the game and one of the three of us would take the loss so she wouldn't have to. A year into this routine, we started to get wise to the fact that 'protecting' her from losing wasn't doing her any favours and we began to have true games, win or lose, with no buffering. It was not a smooth transition. We rode a learning curve which saw Maddy yelling, stomping her feet and crying, and eventually learning to be able to lose comfortably.

Whenever the school had professional development days, I still had to go to work even though the kids were home, so my mom would often come out from Vancouver to watch over Lauren and Maddy. My mom had tremendous patience and staying power and could go six rounds of Trouble and four rounds of Princess Monopoly with only a water break. The one rule my mom had was that if Maddy got upset about losing, the game would be over. These visits were instrumental in Maddy learning how to lose. She desperately wanted to play games with grandma, so she worked her hardest to keep the games going by learning to be a gracious loser.

So much of learning 'with' Madeline was about conditioning. Madeline had always been a good bike rider – another way in which she surpassed glass ceilings imposed by other people. She took pride in her bike-riding abilities and would switch on her 'selective hearing', riding far past us, despite our yelling at her to come back because we had reached the previously decided-upon end point of the bike ride. That all took a turn when she had her hammer toe surgery. She had to learn a different way of riding a bike. We discovered that in order to re-teach her how to ride her bike independently along the public trail near our house, we had to find a way to gradually guide her. Scott and I thought and thought about how we could do it without actually being on Maddy's bike with her and the solution we came up with was the tandem bike.

Scott was the brave one who rode at the front of the bike. That was a tough position to be in because he had to maintain the balance of the bike and do the lion's share of the pedalling. At the beginning, Maddy did not understand the biomechanics of the bike: if she turned to look at a cute dog passing by on the trail, she would cause the bike to go off balance and Scott would have to grip the handle bars and right the bike. Eventually, though, the tandem biking got easier for the two of them. As they rode together, I would ride alongside and explicitly remind Maddy of the safety rules of riding along the trail. Some of the rules were: 'eyes always face forward', 'keep your feet on the pedals', 'stay in the middle of the trail' (going too close to the edge would cause her balance issues), 'go to the parking lot and turn around' and so on. When we 'graduated' from the tandem bike, we still rode with Maddy to keep the 'rules' fresh in her head. She now rides the trail on her own as well and we all feel a great sense of accomplishment that she is independent in that way!

There are so many things that Maddy has achieved in her short life, and some of them seem even more miraculous when you consider that many people can't do the things she can. Lots of people can't ride bikes or ski. Maddy can do both. When Maddy was four, her dad and I envisioned skiing as being a good family activity for the four of us to do and so we decided to teach her how. We didn't know how it would go but we knew we had to try. Using a jerry-rigged system of Mark's worn leather belts with extra holes punched in them to fit her small waist, and ropes to keep her close, we were off to the slopes. It took a couple of years, but eventually Maddy learned how, which to this day completely impresses her doctors.

By the time Maddy was seven, her dad and I had separated, but I wanted to maintain our weekend skiing adventures so I used to try to take the girls out every other weekend during the winter. Sometimes we'd try out new mountain adventures. Once, we drove 90 minutes from our house to Mount Baker in Washington State. I had skied at Mount Baker when I was younger, but the girls had never skied there before. A friend of mine from out of town came along for the adventure and the four of us headed out. Unfortunately, when we got there, I soon realized Maddy was out of her comfort zone. She was fussy and demanding and completely disagreeable. I tried to cajole her out of her mood, but I wasn't reading her signs very well. She was out of her element, skiing a mountain she had never skied before and although we were on the beginner runs, she pushed back at everything we tried. Change was hard for Maddy, and I forgot that. By noon, we decided to call it a day and we were on our last run before heading in. We were crossing under the chair lift with people gliding through the air above us when Maddy fell in some powder. She was tired and she let loose, yelling and screaming, "This is stupid! I can't get up! Help me! Why aren't you helping me?"

When she realized that all the people above us on the chair lift could hear her, she yelled even louder!

It took all my patience and power to remain calm and non-reactive. Eventually, I got her up and we slowly skied to the lodge, got some water and headed to the vehicle. Lesson learned for me: Maddy was quite capable of learning new things, but it had to be a gradual learning curve. I was expecting her to leap like a kangaroo and she was only able to hop like a frog.

Learning from the skiing debacle at Mount Baker, soon thereafter I took Maddy and Lauren to Manning Park. That's where they originally learned to ski and they both felt at ease on that mountain. It was a beautiful spring day. The sun was shining, our goggles were on, our skis were waxed, and we were ready for a great day. The first run was amazing. We got off the orange chair and took our usual route down. On our way off the chair, Lauren noticed a deep tree well just to the right of the chair and she motioned to it so we would notice it and avoid it. And that's all it took to make our second run a completely different story. Once it had been pointed out to her, that tree well drew Maddy in like a bear to honey. It's like the tree had a homing beacon and Maddy was inexplicably drawn to it. Soon enough she had tipped over the edge of the tree well and fallen deep down into it. On that ski trip, I'd brought no friend with us, so it was up to me to hoist a five-foot, two-inch human being with little leg or upper body strength up a tree well. I became increasingly frustrated and sweaty as I tried different ways to get her up and out. First, I tried a 'top down/coach her out' approach. I spoke calmly, giving her literal step-by-step directions.

That didn't work well, as Maddy was unable to visualize what I was asking her to do with her feet and hands.

After a few replications of that approach, I abandoned it for the 'jump right in and lift' approach. It took quite a bit of contorting, heaving and groaning, with Lauren cheering us on from above, before I was able to get her out of the tree well. Maddy and I were both so exhausted when we reached the surface that we just lay in the snow, breathed and stared up at the blue sky for a few minutes before we carried on. I have run many half marathons, done triathlons and skied my whole life, but never before had I sweated so much! It wasn't just because of the physical aspect of the Maddy's retrieval, it was also the emotional aspect; all I could think was, *what the heck do I do if I cannot get her out?*

A couple of years ago, I was preparing for a TEDx talk. Modeled after the more globally-focussed TED (technology, entertainment, design) talks, TEDx brings together local thought leaders, business executives, students and philanthropists. When I was chosen as a speaker, I assumed I could bring notes onto the stage with me. I was sadly mistaken. Even though I'd watched many TED talks in the past, I'd never realized that the speakers did not have notes in their hands. I felt a combination of curiosity and panic when I found out I was expected to speak for 17 minutes without notes.

I have given a lot of workshops in my history as an educator, but I've always had a PowerPoint to support me, or notes to refer to. This TEDx talk opportunity was seriously going to challenge my brain!

The event was three weeks away and Scott could hear me mumbling around the house as I gave my talk to myself while washing dishes, doing laundry, cooking dinner . . . and pretty much any moment I was not in the midst of conversation with anyone. Being the kind man that he is, Scott decided to take Maddy skiing so I could have one day to mumble uninterrupted. Maddy's usual process while skiing with one other person was that she led the route and then someone was behind her so that she could set the pace, and didn't t feel like she was last. The two of them had been skiing one route throughout the day and Maddy was confident and capable on it, but for some reason she decided on a new route that put her behind Scott. The new route consisted of deep piles of powder, which she didn't like skiing in. After a couple of turns, she was down on her butt. Because Scott was ahead of her, it took him some time to get his skis off and climb back to her. Meanwhile, panic had set in and Maddy just started yelling at the first group of people who came by, telling them she needed help getting up. She didn't discriminate about which person would help her—it was going to be the NEXT person down the hill no matter who they were. She was a determined young lady!

Maddy didn't always bring the determination and strong voice she used around strangers to bear on people with whom she was familiar. Shortly after beginning high school, Maddy had an unfortunate incident with a boy who got too close for comfort. After a cooking class, he unnerved her by getting into her personal space, intimidated her and would not move out. That was a situation in which her strong voice would've been welcomed, but it was nowhere to be found. She froze and was unable to speak. Maddy was deeply distressed by this interaction and it took a lot of debriefing, counselling and talking through the incident before she was able to move past it. The situation highlighted her incredible vulnerability when it came to personal space and her inability to self-advocate and be discerning when letting people into her inner circle.

Because of that incident, we participated for six months in a program about assertiveness that was intended to build up Maddy's sense of being so that she could stand up to people who did not have the best intentions, advocate for herself and use her voice. Unfortunately, while in *theory* she was a star student, in *practice*, she had much to learn. When I asked her why she couldn't use her voice to tell people she did not like what they were saying or doing, she said, "I want them to like me and be my friend." That pretty much summed up the futility of the program for us! It wasn't that Maddy *couldn't* learn what to do, it was that her fear of not being liked was bigger.

What we've learned about believing in people's ability to comprehend the world around them is that we must **embrace** each moment of discovery as an opportunity to grow our knowledge, compassion and willingness to be amazed. People will learn differently from each other, but there are no limits to learning.

Conclusion

When Maddy was first going through all her assessments and receiving her diagnoses and subsequent 'labels', the language used was very different from the language we use now.

People used to use the terms, 'autistic kid', or a 'disabled kid' with Maddy. That never sat right with me. It always made my stomach churn—not because people were noting the fact that she had autism, but because the way they referred to her made it feel like they didn't see her as a person at all, that she was just a label to them. I would gently correct everyone and say, "Yes, my child has autism." Thankfully, we have had a cultural shift in our collective mindset that has led to different framing. We no longer put the label first, we put the person first, as it should be! We look at strengths and competencies rather than struggles and deficiencies. People like Shelley Moore, Norman Kunc, Emma Van der Klift, Faye Brownlie and Bruce Beairsto have been on the forefront of building inclusive language, communities and schools in Canada.

Inclusive communities are supportive and enriching to all members.

We all need to ask ourselves what part can we play in disrupting the status quo, to change inequality and inequity to embrace all diversities?

Madeline is a person with autism. *Person* first, *gift* second. People throw the word 'normal' around without thinking about what their intended message is. After each assessment Maddy went through and each diagnosis our family received, inevitably someone would throw the word 'normal' at us in a phrase such as, "It's hard when your kid can't do normal things."

But to us, Maddy *is* normal. Normal is what you are presently living. Normal is your day-to-day. Community creates "normal". Sometimes, normal changes temporarily. For example, if you have braces on your teeth, you must temporarily change the way you eat and clean your teeth for the duration of the time you wear the braces. Other times, our 'normal' changes for the long-term with life events such as illness or accident, job loss or gain, moving house. When someone develops arthritis they need to adapt their activities to their new reality. My personal reality changed when I injured my knee a couple of years ago and could no longer run up mountains; now I walk and do adapted yoga.

Our life with Madeline is normal because it is all that we have ever known. What is the benefit in comparing our 'normal' to someone else's 'normal'? What's 'normal' for us is to make sure each night at dinner we share our gratitude for the day. This gratitude practice keeps us connected to one another's lives, keeps us humble and gives us the opportunity to notice small moments of joy. As a family, we choose to be brave, believe and find laughter even when it is sometimes easier to retreat, question and cry.

The important thing for us is to recognize the humour, humanness and hope we experience each day in getting to live with an amazing person like Madeline!

Lisa Wallace (Kean) is an educator in Chilliwack, British Columbia. She has a master's degree in curriculum and has had the privilege of working in various roles throughout the school district. She embraces the opportunities to learn with and from people every day.

Lisa's 2017 TEDx Chilliwack talk about embracing inclusion and diversity was the impetus for writing this book.

Lisa Kean's TEDx talk: https://www.youtube.com/watch?v=F8ZIpNq1cSQ
Lisa Wallace twitter: @LisaWallaceBC
Lisa Wallace Instagram: lisawallacebc1